Writing and Reporting News You Can Use

Writing and Reporting News You Can Use instructs students on how to produce news stories that are informative, interesting, educational and, most importantly, compelling. It addresses roadblocks to student interest in writing news, using illustrative examples and exercises to help them understand how to write news that is engrossing and accurate. Tammy Trujillo's hands-on approach is based on real-world strategies that deal with audience and market characteristics. Students are writing from the very beginning while also getting the ethical and legal grounding necessary to understand the field. This textbook is a complete resource for students learning broadcast news, including how to get a job after leaving the classroom.

Tammy Trujillo is an award-winning radio news anchor and talk show host with over 30 years' experience in the Los Angeles market and is currently the lead Professor of Broadcasting at Mt. San Antonio College in Walnut, CA, as well as Director of its two campus radio stations. Tammy Trujillo is a member of SAG-AFTRA, a former Board Member of the Associated Press Television and Radio Association, a Hall of Fame member at Long Beach City College and a member of Pacific Pioneer Broadcasters.

Writing and Reporting News You Can Use

Tammy Trujillo

Routledge
Taylor & Francis Group
NEW YORK AND LONDON

First published 2018
by Routledge
711 Third Avenue, New York, NY 10017

and by Routledge
2 Park Square, Milton Park, Abingdon, Oxon, OX14 4RN

Routledge is an imprint of the Taylor & Francis Group, an informa business

© 2018 Taylor & Francis

The right of Tammy Trujillo to be identified as author of this work has been asserted by her in accordance with sections 77 and 78 of the Copyright, Designs and Patents Act 1988.

All rights reserved. No part of this book may be reprinted or reproduced or utilised in any form or by any electronic, mechanical, or other means, now known or hereafter invented, including photocopying and recording, or in any information storage or retrieval system, without permission in writing from the publishers.

Trademark notice: Product or corporate names may be trademarks or registered trademarks, and are used only for identification and explanation without intent to infringe.

Library of Congress Cataloging-in-Publication Data
A catalog record for this book has been requested

ISBN: 978-1-138-28424-1 (hbk)
ISBN: 978-1-138-28427-2 (pbk)
ISBN: 978-1-315-26963-4 (ebk)

Typeset in Optima
by Apex CoVantage, LLC

Contents

Acknowledgments   xi
Preface   xii

PART I: INTRODUCTION   1
First, We Need to Know Where News Comes From!   5

PART II: THE BASICS   7

1. **What is News and Where Does It Come From?**   9
   Different Types of News   10
   Reactions to News   12
   Wire Services   13
   Audio and Video Services   13

2. **What Do People Want from a Newscast?**   17
   Information   18
   Relevancy   18
   Education   19
   Entertainment   21

3. **The Rules and Regulations – Avoiding Legal Problems**   24
   Libel, Defamation and Slander   26
   False Light   27
   Plugola   28

Contents

Attribution 29
Identification of Minors 30
Fair Use Law 31

4. Ethical and Moral Newswriting 34
Professional Ethics 35
Unbiased Reporting 40
Fair and Balanced Reporting 41
Dealing with Victims of Tragedy 41
Editorializing 43

PART III: TIME TO WRITE 47

5. News Judgment – How to Pick the Right Stories 49
Selecting Stories 49
Understanding Audience Dynamics 50
Deciding on Your Lead Story 51

6. Writing the News 53
Conversational Writing – Write Like You Talk 55
Style Points 56
Working with Wire Copy 60
Writing from Press Releases 61
Answer the Question 62

7. Re-write and Then Re-write It Again 65
Pronouncers 66
Proof Reading – Mistakes and Clarity 69
Writing Multiple Sides 71

8. Types of Stories 76
Readers 77
Actuality Stories 78
Wraps 78
To Follows 78
Reax 79
Question and Answer 80

Contents

Man on the Street 80
Kicker Stories 80
Writing for Time 81

9. Teases, Promos and Headlines   **83**
Promos 84
Teases 84
Headlines 85
How Far is Too Far? 86

10. Enterprising Stories   **90**
Finding Ideas 91
Sourcing the Story 92
Relevance to the Audience 93

11. Creating Series or Multi-part Stories   **95**
Purpose and Benefits 95
Outlining the Story 96
Developing the Story 97
Finding Expert Interviews 98
Formatting the Story 99
Recapping the Previous Segment 99

12. Public Affairs and Public Service Announcements   **102**
FCC Requirements 103
The Public File 104
Working with Ascertained Issues 104
Finding Interesting Topics and Guests 105
Preparing for the Interview 105
Post-show Responsibilities 106
Public Service Announcements 107
The Quarterly Report 108

13. Other Types of News   **110**
Sports 111
Business 114
Traffic 114
Weather 116

vii

Contents

PART IV: WORKING WITH AUDIO AND VIDEO   **119**

14. Types of Audio and Video   **121**
Proper Use of Audio and Video   *122*
Wire-generated Audio and Video   *122*
Station-gathered Audio and Video   *124*
Ambient Sound and B-Roll   *125*

15. Effective Interviewing   **128**
Preparing for the Interview   *129*
Make It Interesting   *131*
Asking the Right Questions   *132*
Asking the Hard Questions   *134*
Getting Too Much Information   *134*

16. Selecting and Writing with Interview Clips   **138**
Finding the Right Cut   *139*
Writing In and Out of Cuts for Radio   *140*
Working In and Around Cuts for Television   *143*
Working with Multiple Cuts   *144*
Getting Information from the Interview   *144*
Using Ambient Sound   *144*

PART V: SOCIAL AND MULTI-MEDIA NEWS   **149**

17. Writing for Internet Usage   **151**
Style Differences   *152*
Content Curation   *152*
Spotting Fake News Sites   *153*
Proper Attribution   *154*
Links to Other Media   *154*
Accuracy, Reliability and Responsibility   *155*

18. Packaging for Multi-media   **158**
Online Audio and Video   *159*
Use of Stills   *160*
Podcasts   *160*
RSS Feeds   *162*

Contents

19. Social Media as a News Source   **164**
The Role of Social Media 166
Validating Social Media and Proper Vetting 167
Legal Considerations 168
Promotion Through Social Media 168

PART VI: PRESENTING THE NEWS   **171**

20. The Right Attitude and Approach   **173**
Understanding the Story 174
The Delivery 174
Attitude Changes During the Newscast 176

21. Looking Like a Pro   **179**
Professionalism 180
Looking the Part 181
Personal Choices 182

PART VII: BECOMING A PRO   **185**

22. The Life of a News Professional   **187**
On-call and 24/7 Schedules 187
Stress and Emotions 188
Travel and Relocating 189
Family Life 189

23. Creating and Marketing Your Demo   **192**
Cover Letters and Resumes 192
Creating Material 194
Websites 194
Internet Presence 195
Branding and Marketing 195

24. News Tests and Interviews   **198**
Preparing for the Interview 198
Being a Successful Interviewee 199
News Tests 200
Follow-up 201

Contents

25. Making Your First Career Move **203**
Research 203
Geographical Considerations 204
Unions, Agents and Managers 205

PART VIII: CONCLUSION **207**
Sense of Duty 209
Pursuing Your Passion 210
Rewards of Being a News Professional 210

About the Author 215
Index 217

Acknowledgments

This book is dedicated to all the hard-working, ethical and committed people who work to bring the public the news on a daily basis. Few of us make the headlines and we are not supposed to. We are never supposed to be part of the story. But at the scene of news, we see and feel and hear what happens just as anyone would and it can have a profound impact days, months and even years later. It takes stamina, curiosity, skill, tenacity, composure and compassion to work in the news industry. We are there 24/7 to bring the public the information it needs, at times even putting our very lives in danger to do it. I am proud to be part of this community and proud of every man and woman who is a part of it as well.

A special thanks to all the awesome news pros who provided the many quotes that appear throughout this book. Your insight, candor and, in some cases, humor are very much appreciated!

Preface

I never thought that I would be a newscaster, traffic reporter or sportscaster. In fact, graduating high school, I wasn't sure what I wanted to be. I looked into a lot of things, finally settling on teaching elementary school as a career. Not really because I wanted to, but it was one of those traditional jobs for girls to go into. So, I got my degree and thought that my future was set. One semester, and my mind was changed. That was *not* what I wanted for the rest of my working life.

So what to do! I took a look at my skills and what I liked. I liked music, liked to talk and had endured professional voice training as a child, so I had a good voice. To me, it all seemed to add up to becoming a disc jockey. So, I found a program, got my training and landed my first job, fortunately in Southern California where I grew up and home to the second largest market in the nation, Los Angeles.

Unfortunately, I found out rather quickly that I was not funny or interesting and really didn't have much to say. But I liked being behind the mic and thought that if I actually had something to say, this would be a very good career. So I made the switch to something that came with its own scripts and content... news.

I had never liked the news. My mom always had it on in the kitchen and I found the people doing it to be boring and the news to be even more uninteresting. Now though, faced with doing it myself, I realized I had to find a way to like it if I was going to enjoy and be successful in my new career.

At first, I simply read wire copy on the air. Gradually, I started experimenting with rewriting it so that if the story wasn't particularly interesting, it at least sounded like I was just relaying the information, instead of

Preface

announcing it from the top of the mountain. I started finding ways to select stories that were actually important and to write them in a way that made that relevance obvious to the listeners. And I started finding fun, bizarre and sometimes even silly stories to use at the end of my newscasts so that there wasn't such an awkward transition back to the rock music that the radio station on my first job was playing.

It has been that approach that has fueled my career. In fact, I think it may be one of the main reasons that I have had and continue to have a successful one. When I meet people I hear things like, "You told me about . . ." or "I really feel like I already know you . . .". That is the key; making people feel like you are simply talking just to them and not to the millions of people out there in the audience.

I did go back and get my degree in Communications and, in addition to working full-time on the air, started teaching college courses pretty early in my career. For many years, I have been frustrated with the books that I have had to choose from for my newswriting and reporting classes. Don't get me wrong, they are well-written and contain a lot of good information, but they don't teach students how to connect with the audience, how to choose stories that matter, how to make them relate to the audience and to have fun doing it in the process.

Most also don't really address how to do sports, weather, traffic and business . . . all things that are often required of a newscaster or reporter and all things that I had to teach myself.

So, after the success of my first book, *Intern Insider – Getting the Most of your Internship in the Entertainment Field* (Focal Press, 2016), I decided that I would write the book that I had always wished I had to use in my classes and make it one that would include everything that I have learned through my own career.

Much has changed since I got started in the industry. Today, we are able to reach people no matter where they are. They no longer need to be in front of a radio or television set. We are right in the palm of their hands on smartphones and tablets. And that gives us the opportunity to be an even bigger part of their lives and to impact their lives in ways we never before were able to.

News can be much more than just letting people know what is going on. You can enrich their lives with information about what is happening in their communities and how it affects them, you can let them know about

xiii

Preface

opportunities, you can entertain them . . . and in times of disaster, you may even help save a life.

To me, there is not much more that a person could want from a career.

I hope you enjoy using this book in your class. And I hope it helps to change any impression that you might have that news is boring. It can be, but it does not have to be. You can make sure that it isn't. Good luck in your career. I hope you have as good a time as I have had!

PART I

Introduction

Source: tulpahn/shutterstock.com

Introduction

In this Chapter

- Why Most Students Don't Listen to or Watch the News
- Where the News Comes From
- What Makes News Appear Boring
- What Can be Done to Make it Interesting
- What Students Will Learn From the Book

Boring, irrelevant, negative . . . some of the words used by students to explain why they don't watch or listen to the news. And often, they're not totally wrong.

News is primarily negative. That's a fact. And unfortunately, the more negative a story is, the more attention it is likely to get. Sadly, that means that listeners have become accustomed to thinking that if a story isn't mostly negative in nature, it's not news. There's an awful phrase used in newsrooms, "If it bleeds, it leads". Awful, but true.

As News Director at a Los Angeles radio station in the 1990s, we decided to try something different. I realized that when people woke up to us on their clock alarm, there we were, starting their day off with "doom, gloom, death and destruction". What a way to wake up! Kind of makes you want to pull the covers back over your head and just hide in bed all day.

So we decided to start our twice-an-hour newscasts with a positive story. Not a silly or funny story, but one about something that wasn't negative. There are plenty of them out there. Hero stories, stories about medical breakthroughs, people being successful, etc. My morning show partner

Introduction

and I certainly began enjoying our newscasts more. And we thought our listeners were too.

That is, until we started getting letters and faxes (remember, this is the mid-1990s; emails and texts are still some years off). People wanted to know why I was no longer doing the news!

We've been taught that the first story of the newscast is supposed to be the most important one going on at the moment. And in most models, it should be. But in our case, people were hearing a positive story and, because of conditioning, didn't see it as important. And, in as much, they thought that if *that* story was the most important one of the cast, then the rest of the stories would be far less important. Many told us that because of that, they were tuning out and going elsewhere on the dial for their morning news.

Two big rules in broadcasting . . . get them there and then keep them there! We were a very popular station, so we were getting the listeners . . . but we were also letting them get away by not meeting their expectations. So, our experiment was over. We went back to opening the news with "doom, gloom, death and destruction". And everyone was happy . . . or were they?

Remember, one of our biggest complaints, not just from students, but from people in general, is that news is negative!

So what do we do?

Source: Microgen/shutterstock.com

Introduction

First, We Need to Know Where News Comes From!

How do radio and TV stations find the stories that eventually end up in their newscasts?

Much of what is heard and seen in television and radio news is taken straight from one of several wire services. Two of the biggest are the Associated Press and Reuters. These companies churn out news; local, national and international, non-stop, 24 hours a day, seven days a week. They also cover sports, weather, business and entertainment. There is a lot of material and a lot of it is negative. And a lot of it also might seem irrelevant to your listeners.

These stories are often written quickly and are written not only for the electronic news media, but also for published news outlets such as newspapers.

That's part of the problem. The writing styles between the two mediums are quite different. If someone takes a story that is written for publication and reads it on the air verbatim, chances are the story is going to sound very unnatural and stilted. It needs to be re-written in a style that lends itself to the spoken word as opposed to being read silently.

The stories are written in a variety of lengths. Some are very short, 15–20 seconds. It's hard to really tell a complete story in that amount of time. Others are much longer, possibly as long as two to three minutes.

News writers work on many, many stories a day . . . sometimes upwards of 80 to 100 a shift at a 24-hour-a-day news radio station. And in moving that fast, sometimes wire copy is not re-written or only very lightly re-written. And if information isn't in the piece of wire copy that was assigned to a writer to use to create a story, it often doesn't end up in the script for air either, so the relevance of the story to the audience may be lost.

The wire services cover the big stories. That's their job. They're trying to please everyone . . . all the different entities and companies that subscribe to their services. They hit the major stories of the day. They handle the biggest of the regional stories. And when it comes to stories local to an area, they cover only the biggest of those as well. So the smaller stories, the ones that might be important or of interest to local neighborhoods or groups, don't show up.

Introduction

So with all that said, what is there to do? **How do we make news interesting, informative and yes, even entertaining?** In other words, how do we create "News You Can Use" (and want to listen to)?

It takes some work, thinking, creativity and artistry.

It all starts with knowing your audience. If you are putting together a newscast for the students who listen to your college radio or TV station, a story about cuts in Medicare shouldn't be in it.

It's an important story, just not to your audience. In this scenario, it's a 'who cares story', one that will cause most of your listeners to tune out.

Just because a story is on the wire service doesn't mean it necessarily belongs in your newscast. You need to keep your audience in mind when you sort through the massive amount of news coming down from the wire services. You want to select stories that will matter to your audience. And it's a guarantee that all of them will not.

What are the people in your listening audience talking about? That's also news, even though it might not be on the wires. You need to decide what's in your newscast, don't let the wire services do that for you. There are many sources for story ideas, including your own life and the lives of the other people at the station.

Just because a story isn't on the wire service doesn't mean it's not news! It simply may be a story that the wires didn't pick up. Think outside the box! Using personal, everyday experiences to create news stories can make your newscasts more relative and interesting to your audience. And you'll have stories on your air that the other local stations don't . . . making your station and your newscasts stand out.

"News You Can Use" is about making sure that while we still cover the "doom, gloom, death and destruction" that unfortunately makes up the bulk of the news and is what our listeners expect from us, we also are making sure that every story counts.

In this book, we will focus on creating stories and newscasts that still cover the important stories and events but can no longer be called 'irrelevant or boring'. We'll learn how to ask the hard questions during an interview and get amazing audio and video that will bring the story into focus while making listeners care. We'll find ways to 'color' stories with natural or ambient sound and music, sound effects and other production elements.

So forget what you think about the news and join me in creating "News You Can Use".

PART

The Basics

What is News and Where Does It Come From?

In this Chapter

- Different Types of News
- Reactions to News
- Wire Services
- Audio and Video Services

Increase Your Industry Vocabulary

- AP – Associated Press, one of the largest news-gathering and disseminating companies in the world
- International – Covering the world, from any country
- Kicker – A fun or entertaining story, usually used to end the newscast on a positive note or can be used as a bridge between news stories and sports and weather
- Local – A story from the area mainly served by the radio or TV station, usually covers several counties
- National – A story originating from somewhere in the United States
- Regions/Regional – A story that comes from the geographic region the radio or TV station covers such as the Southwest, Northwest, Midwest or East Coast

The Basics

- Reuters – An international news agency headquartered in London that covers international news, business, politics and other news

- Wire service – A news agency that supplies news materials to newspapers, radio and television stations

As we said in the Introduction, most people think that to qualify as news, a story has to be about "doom, gloom, death and destruction". After all, that is how many news outlets program their news. And unfortunately, there are a lot of negative things that happen in the world that need to be covered. But there are certainly a lot of other stories out there as well that can and often deserve to be covered in our news reporting.

One of the key goals in anything that we program on the air is to get a reaction from our audience. A well-written story should create some sort of feeling in our viewers or listeners. If it doesn't, then we need to question why that story is taking up our airtime.

The majority of radio and TV stations that program news subscribe to services that report from all over the world. They provide the copy, audio and even video for these subscribing stations to either simply use as-is on the air or to use as material to create their own versions of the stories.

But they cannot cover every single story that happens each day, especially the smaller stories that may not make a difference on a national or even regional level, but are often of great importance to our local communities. It takes effort to find these stories and include them to create a balanced and valuable newscast for our audiences.

Different Types of News

There is no perfect answer to the question "What is news?" News basically is anything that happens that is of interest to your audience. Sometimes the most important story of the day is of a national level; sometimes it is international. It can also be local or it can even be a human-interest story or something from the world of entertainment.

Stories come in a variety of categories:

1. Stories that are of mass appeal and general interest. These are the top issues of the day that have the potential to interest a broad segment of the population. They might include politics, new laws or crime stories.

What is News and Where Does It Come From?

2. Stories that are educational or informative. These are stories that contain information that the public needs to know. They might include details on evacuations during a wildfire or storm, a crime story that generates a warning for the public or perhaps a story on a medical breakthrough.
3. Stories that are simply interesting or entertaining. These stories often fall into the category of 'kickers' or human-interest stories; the more light-hearted stories that we often try to end a newscast with. They can include entertainment-related or humorous stories or feel-good stories like one about a local hero who makes good. They may be as small as a story about who won the local spelling bee, depending, of course, upon the size of the market you are in.

A well-constructed newscast will have a mix of all three types of stories. The numbers of each, of course, depend on what is going on in the world on any given day.

Stories about crimes almost always seem to dominate the news unless something else pushes its way into that prime first story spot. Why crime? Crime is something that most people are either interested in or concerned about. People want to feel safe and in a crime story, they can take solace in the fact that the suspect has been arrested or get the information they need to try and protect themselves, such as in a description of whoever police are looking for. Crime is something that everyone understands. In other words, your audience gets the relevance of the story even if it is not in their immediate neighborhood.

That's why crime stories are often the ones 'teased' in the run-ups to the newscast. Because if we say something like "The pair who have been hitting banks throughout the city has been captured", or "The killer of joggers in the park has another victim", it's a pretty sure bet that you will stick around to hear the story.

Whenever we talk about the media, it is important to remember that while its goal is to inform viewers, listeners and readers about what's going on in the world, it is still a business. And the goal of any business is to make money. So while we strive to put together informative and entertaining newscasts, we also need to constantly be aware of what the audience wants and make sure we service those needs. This translates into viewers and listeners and that translates into ratings and profits.

So while crime stories are always a sure bet to lead the news, there certainly can be exceptions. During the 2016 presidential campaign and

The Basics

certainly following the subsequent election, news from the White House was front and center for quite a while. In some cases, it was the lead story even in cities where there *was* a big crime-related story or other important story that normally would have been what we call a lead-all or a story that would have topped all the newscasts and/or news cycles.

Natural disasters or extreme weather are also good candidates to take over the lead story slot. Again, these are the kinds of stories where the public turns to the media for up-to-the-minute information and advice on what to do. It's always comforting to have someone – even if it is only a person on the radio or television – to help you through a frightening time. It is during such events that we, as broadcasters, actually have a chance to increase the loyalty of our listeners if we just keep in mind what they need and what they are feeling and make sure we provide the appropriate information.

 Reactions to News

The stories that we include in our newscasts can cause a variety of reactions among our listeners and viewers. Getting a reaction should always be your goal when selecting, writing and presenting a story. Key reactions include:

- Wow, I didn't know that!
- That's happened to me!
- That's interesting!

The reaction you don't want is:

- Who cares?

Sadly, too often that is the reaction to at least several of the stories in any given newscast. It's one that is actually very easy to avoid. We will talk about avoiding 'who cares' news in Chapter 2.

We want the audience to feel that they have gotten something from our newscasts. That is the key to keeping them tuning in. No one is going to come back to a station or program if they feel they have just wasted a half hour listening to news that they didn't care about.

With stations now actively using social media as part of their news effort, it is likely that you will be very quickly aware of your audience's reaction to your stories. Some stations even encourage their anchors and reporters to interact with viewers and listeners concerning the stories on their air.

Wire Services

Most newsrooms across the country subscribe to one or more wire services. These are news agencies that provide syndicated news online to newspapers, radio and TV stations.

AP, or the Associated Press, is the largest of the wire services. Its reporters cover everything from large local stories to regional, national and international news. They cover general news as well as specialties such as sports, entertainment, business and weather.

Reuters is another of the bigger wire services. It specializes in news from all over the world with a special emphasis on business, politics, entertainment and technology.

There are many smaller wire services that will cover stories on a much more local level and may only deal with one or two regions.

Stations can customize what they receive in several ways. Some stations only take the written copy and will either read it verbatim on the air or have writers re-write the information into new versions, or sides, of the story. Because the stations subscribe to the wire service, they are allowed to read the copy exactly as it comes over the air without any possible copyright infringement. Even though, it is not a best practice to read wire copy without at least some rewriting, except in a true emergency situation. This way you can make sure the story is written in a conversational style and you will make it unique to your station.

Audio and Video Services

With the larger wire services, they also offer stations audio clips from newsmakers. Everything from actualities or sound bites from interviews to stories that are totally self-contained and filed by their own reporters.

The Basics

Subscribing stations can use the actualities to create their own stories or pull the complete stories to use on their air, giving listeners the impression that they have their own team of reporters and that they are widespread across the country.

Video services are also available through many of the wire services. Just as with the audio, stations are able to pull cuts to put into stories written by their own reporters or use fully packaged stories to include in their newscasts. Again, because the wire services require a subscription, the stations can freely use these resources without any additional fees, credit or concerns about copyright.

The stories are delivered from the wire services via a news platform and there are quite a few of these on the market. Among the most popular are NewsBoss, AP Newsdesk, Burli and ENPS. These platforms are capable of bringing in a number of wire services at the same time and sorting the stories by category. Some also contain digital editors so that audio or video can be easily manipulated by a reporter or writer right at their desks in the newsroom without the need for them to go to a separate production studio.

Most also have the capability for an editor to create an entire newscast in the platform and send it directly to the anchor who can then fire the corresponding audio or video elements while on the air by simply hitting the '0' key on the numeric pad on their keyboard.

Points to Remember

- Not all news is negative. A good newscast contains a variety of different types of stories.

- The wire services provide the material for much of our newscasts, but not all stories that come down the wire service are suitable for use in your market or for your audience's demographic.

- The wire services are not the only source of information or ideas for stories. Press releases, things you see or hear about that are going on in your community or even your own experiences can also make great stories.

- Every story should matter. Stories that make you think 'who cares' should not be included in a newscast.

14

Exercises

One of the best ways you can learn how to write news stories and create effective newscasts is to listen to your local radio and TV stations. Hopefully, you are already doing this on a regular basis. It is also a good idea for you to go outside your comfort zone and check out stations that you normally wouldn't watch or listen to. When it comes to getting that first job, or even other positions along the way, you want to be able to apply to the widest range of stations, not just those that play your favorite type of music or present the news in exactly the way you like.

1. Listen or watch a radio or TV newscast. During the newscast, categorize the stories according to the following list and write your one- or two-word reaction to each one of them. Do not include sports.

    ● General interest

    ● Informative

    ● Kicker

2. Select one of the stories that you included in Exercise 1 and answer the following questions:

    ● What is the topic of the story?

    ● Why would this story matter to the audience?

    ● What kind of reaction would you expect them to have?

    I learned three VERY valuable lessons to guide you. Ask yourself when you write, produce, report or anchor:

    1) What happened?

    2) Who cares?

    3) What do we see or hear?

    —Mary Lyon – former Associated Press
    Radio Network – West Coast Entertainment Reporter,
    former Writer/Reporter/Producer – KTLA-TV,
    NBC Radio, KRTH, KHJ, KLOS, KNAC,
    KLOS – Los Angeles

The Basics

We all carry a certain amount of bias with us but if you want to call yourself a journalist, then you will, to the very best of your ability, leave your bias at home on the doorstep when you go in for work. If you can't do that, then go do something else.

—Ron Olsen – KTLA/KABC, Retired

What Do People Want from a Newscast?

2

In this Chapter

- Information – Things that are going on
- Relevancy – How do these things affect me or why are they important to me?
- Education – Things the audience needs to know
- Entertainment – Things that are fun or interesting

Increase Your Industry Vocabulary

- Relevant – Stories and information appropriate and of interest to your audience
- Water cooler story – Another word for a kicker story

Most people do not watch or listen to the news for entertainment. They are seeking something. They may be there because they seriously want to know what went on in the world today and how it may affect them. They may be there to get traffic reports so they don't get stuck on the freeway on their way to or from work. They may want sports or stock updates. Whatever it is that brought them to the newscast, it is our job to fulfill their needs and in doing so keep them tuned in for as long as possible.

We can do that by providing the correct stories for our demographic, writing them in a conversational, accurate and informative manner and delivering them with professionalism and personality. If we are able to do

The Basics

these things, we very likely will make that listener or viewer a return consumer of our product and that is exactly what we are there to do.

There was a time when people had very limited options on where and how to get their news and information. It basically boiled down to the newspaper, radio or TV. That is not the case today. People don't have to go any further than their cellphones that are nearly almost always in their hands to find out what is going on. So we are faced with the challenge of how to make them put down the phone and tune us in.

The key is understanding what people want from a newscast . . . and making sure to give it to them.

Information

This is probably the number one reason that people tune into the news on an average day. They simply want to know what is going on. Many probably don't expect that any of the stories will directly affect them, but they are curious about what's happening.

The horrific events of September 11, 2001 changed many people's views of what constituted their world. Suddenly, we were focused on other countries in a way that we hadn't really been since World War II when most people felt the need to try and keep an eye on the entire world. But of course, that was during a time when access to information was very limited.

Since then, with the growth of the Internet and the continued intertwining of social media and the news, people are much more in tune with what is happening worldwide. There's a lot of news generated each day and it is up to us to sort it out and select the stories that will be most important and have the most impact for our listeners and then serve those stories up in a way that is both informative and professional.

Relevancy

Every story that makes it onto the air needs to pass the 'who cares' test. What that means is after the story, you do not want the listener or viewer to say 'who cares'. If a story truly is one that no one in your audience will care about, then it shouldn't be in your newscast. Every second you are on the air has a dollar value to it. Airtime is valuable; too valuable to be wasted on a story that will not impact your audience.

But the relevancy of a story is not always that obvious. The story might have real importance to the audience, but if it's not immediately clear, we need to add that into the story. You want your audience to understand why they are hearing or seeing this story.

For example, let's say we have a story about a quarter-percent increase in property taxes. If we just put in the facts as they probably come down from the wire services, all the audience knows is that property taxes are going up. Ok, but the real impact of the story is how much? Don't make your audience do the math, the majority won't. Adding a line like "that means an additional $x per one-thousand-dollars of a home's value" or "that means an increase of $x on a home valued at 500-thousand-dollars" makes the story matter to your audience. They now know exactly why they should care.

Often, writers, reporters and anchors are hesitant to add anything to wire copy. Sometimes they aren't aware that they even can. They simply rewrite and restate what the copy already says. While that might be fine in many cases, in stories such as this one, the copy benefits greatly from some additional information. It is absolutely worth taking the extra time to figure out and add in these details.

Education

We are not talking about education in the traditional sense. The audience is not looking to us to teach them things. But they are looking to us to give them information on things that they need to know.

This is especially true in times of crisis or emergency, like an earthquake or a brush fire, and particularly with radio.

During a disaster such as an earthquake, it is very likely that the power will go out and cellphone service and Internet service might as well, meaning that a battery powered radio, a radio station app or the car radio will be the only sources of news. And during something like a brush fire or flood, where people are being forced to evacuate, they will likely be in the car with the radio close at hand.

Your audience will need information quickly on things like where the problems are centered, road closures, evacuations, safety tips, etc. Even

The Basics

if cellphones and the Internet are working, in emergency situations, most people won't have the time or want to spend it searching through a variety of websites. They want the information they need quickly, easily and clearly. It's during this type of situation that we can really shine. Figure out what people need to know, keep it updated, air it concisely and you can have a listener or viewer for life.

A number of years ago, a major brush fire was sweeping through the foothills in Southern California. Homes were being destroyed in the hundreds and thousands of people were being evacuated. And, the fire continued to burn out of control.

One of my graduates was working as an overnight board operator at a radio station close to the fire. She could see it from the station although she was not in any danger. Her job was just to push the buttons and make sure the station stayed on the air, but the phones kept ringing with people near the fire asking her for information on what they should do or people trying to find out the status of family and friends. They called the radio station because they were used to it being the place they went for information and even though this was a music-intensive station, they were desperately looking to help.

My former student started looking up the information on the Internet and relaying it to callers. After a couple of hours of doing this, she made a very bold move. She started going on the microphone between songs and dropping in the info she had gathered. She was not supposed to talk over the air at all, but she felt so compelled to get the information that the station's listeners needed so badly out to them that she broke a cardinal rule for a board op.

She spent the next day waiting for a phone call she knew in all likelihood would be coming. She fully anticipated losing her board op job. Her program director did call and asked her to come down to the station for a meeting. But instead of firing her, he showed her the faxes and emails they had been getting throughout the day from listeners thanking her and the station for helping them get through what had been a terrifying night. Talk about loyal listeners. They had turned to the station with their needs and the station had responded.

Instead of being fired, my former student was told that she was now free to go on mic and actually jock the overnight shifts from now on. She had done the right thing for the situation, proving she knew what her listeners wanted and needed and how to provide it even though she had broken a very important rule.

Now, I am not suggesting that you want to make a practice of breaking the rules at your radio or TV station. It was a risky thing for my former student to do and could have cost her the first paying job of her career. But it does illustrate clearly that people depend on us, especially in highly stressful times and that if we provide them with what they need in these cases, we will be able to have an important impact on people's lives and in turn gain the loyalty of the audience.

Entertainment

Doom, gloom, death and destruction. We've already established that unfortunately these topics make up the bulk of the stories in our newscasts. But there is always room for something fun or entertaining.

Usually these stories are reserved for near the end of the newscast. Not only do people seem to feel that they don't belong in an earlier position in our line-ups, but by putting the stories lower in the cast, they serve to end the newscast on a lighter note. That makes it much easier to get back into the music if your newscast is airing on a radio station or to go into other programming if you're doing a television news program.

Quite a variety of stories can go under this heading such as:

- Entertainment stories about awards, new movies, music, celebrity news, etc.
- Human interest stories such as the birth of an animal at the local zoo or the latest on a big lottery winner
- Silly or amusing stories like the bank robber who writes his "give me money" note for the teller on the back of his electricity bill

Stories like this are called kickers but are also often called 'water cooler' stories because they are the type of stories that people are likely to share with friends or co-workers at the water cooler or in the breakroom. When these stories are repeated, the question of "where did you hear that?" is often asked. The naming of your station as the source is great publicity.

The Basics

Points to Remember

- People tune into the news looking for something. They have a need, whether it is information on what is going on in the world, region or in their local community, sports, weather, business, etc.
- You need to understand your audience in order to select stories that will interest them.
- Not every detail that you need in a story may be included in the wire copy version of that story. You may need or want to add other details.
- The stories that we choose can have a very vital impact on our audience.
- In times of crisis or emergency, you can provide a very important service to your viewers and listeners.

Exercises

1. What information do you think your audience would want included in the following stories?
   - An earthquake
   - A sales tax increase
   - A road or street closure
   - A new law
   - A food product recall
   - A new airline serving your local airport

2. Using the following stories, find a way to make them relevant to your audience. As they are, while the stories are of value in your newscast, their impact is not clear. Look for ways to make your audience understand what the stories mean to them.
   - It's going to cost more to own your home next year. Property taxes in South County are going up 1.3 percent. Local authorities say they need the additional revenue. You'll see the increase included on the bill that will be due next April.

What Do People Want from a Newscast?

- Starting in March, you'll be able to ride the train further. Metro Rail's train service will cut the ribbon on its five-mile extension. It's something that city leaders have said has been needed for some time. The extension was funded by a bond measure approved by voters back in 2015.

- Banks are getting tougher about bounced checks. The federal government has changed the rules on how much banks can charge people who write bad checks. It's also increased the amount that a recipient of a bad check can get if they take the writer to court. The percentage of bank customers who write bad checks has increased since the 2008 recession.

Your job as a reporter is to understand complicated issues and explain them to the public. I appreciated that as a news reporter at KGB FM & AM in San Diego, but I appreciate journalists work even more now as a newsmaker myself, five-term Councilmember and former Mayor of Santa Monica. Journalists are as important to a functioning democracy as legislators.

—Kevin McKeown

Almost anyone can be taught the mechanics of building a newscast. Knowing what's important to your audience . . . to your market . . . and being able to effectively communicate it . . . that's where the fun comes. And the gratification. In other words, pay attention to the psychology of news, not just the process.

—Roger Nadel – SVP/Affiliate Operations,
Total Traffic & Weather Network; former GM,
KFWB-AM Los Angeles and WWJ-AM Detroit

3 The Rules and Regulations – Avoiding Legal Problems

In this Chapter

- Libel, Defamation and Slander
- False Light
- Plugola
- Attribution
- Identification of Minors
- Fair Use Law

Increasing Your Industry Vocabulary

- Attribution – Referencing the source of a news story or any information contained in that story
- Defamation – Damaging the reputation of a person or company either in writing or verbally
- Endorsements – When an on-air personality uses their name and position to promote a product, company or service
- Fair Use – A set of rules that allow a copyrighted work to be used without the permission of the copyright holder
- False Light – Creating a false impression of someone through the improper use of audio or video

The Rules and Regulations

- Libel – Publishing a false statement or story that damages the reputation of a person or company

- Plugola – The practice of taking money, products, gifts or services for putting a story or information on the air without the involvement of the station

- Slander – Making a false statement that damages the reputation of a person or company

- Testimonial – When an on-air personality promotes a product, company or service by telling about their personal experience and satisfaction with it

Accuracy must be your primary concern when writing and reporting the news. You have a great deal of power when you are on the microphone or on camera or writing the material that the on-air talent will present. It is very easy to permanently do serious harm to someone if you are not careful and do not double-check your facts before putting negative information about someone on the air.

We work very fast in the news industry and sometimes you will find there are mere minutes between the time you write something and it hitting the air. There will be mistakes. We are human. If they happen, they need to be corrected; immediately and prominently.

Being careless, rushing, doing a sloppy job of fact-checking, or because of a personal bias against someone or something is not only unethical, it can also result in legal problems, not just for the station but for you as an individual as well.

We are not only putting our information over the airwaves today but also on the Internet. We need to make sure that we take the same care and concern about accuracy when we create a story for publication on websites, blogs or on social media.

This includes not only the station's sites, but on your personal sites as well. Even if you are acting as a personal individual, the public likely will continue to see you as a news professional and your actions could not only reflect on you in that capacity but also on the station where you work.

It's important to remember that as a broadcast news professional you are no longer just a regular member of the community. People look up to

25

The Basics

you, rely on you and have confidence in you, whether you are acting in your professional role or not.

 ## Libel, Defamation and Slander

Much of our work revolves around reporting on people and there are laws that protect the people and organizations that are involved in the stories that we cover. Defamation is the action of damaging the character or good reputation of an individual or a group by spreading false information about them. Libel pertains to doing this in writing, while slander protects someone from injury by something that is spoken. Even with this difference, the two forms of protection operate the same. They are often simply referred to as defamation.

To be covered by these laws, the information has to be false. If it is true, then defamation laws will not apply. And it is important to note that these laws don't just apply to individuals but also to groups and organizations as well.

Defamation laws vary between the states, so each time you take a job in a new state you need to make yourself aware of that state's laws. If the station you are working for does not make them available, it is your job as a responsible media professional to find them out for yourself. Not knowing the law does not make you immune from being prosecuted for defaming someone.

Again, if the information that you are reporting is true, no matter how negative it might be about a group or individual, then you have nothing to worry about. But you can be sued if what you write or report meets the following criteria:

- The statement is false.
- It has damaged a person or group's reputation or good name.
- Hurt feelings do not count. The result of the damage must be calculable, such as the loss of a job, earnings or if it causes the person to be excluded by people in their circle.
- It can be proven that the station, the writer or the reporter involved was negligent. In other words, the fact the information was flawed could have been discovered if the station or employee had done more research.

The Rules and Regulations

- The reporter or writer knew that the information would damage the person or group and went through with the broadcast anyway. This could be construed as malice.

There are some exceptions to these conditions. If a reporter or writer is quoting something that is said during a legislative session or during a court proceeding, they cannot be sued. This would also apply to quoting anything from a document that is in the public domain. This protection is called 'privilege'.

The other is what is known as 'fair comment'. It generally applies to people who are in the public eye and would include actors, athletes, lawmakers and people in other types of positions that often are the source of news stories. It allows the media to criticize, critique and examine their words and actions without fear of legal reprisal unless that reporting is done with the express intent of damaging the person's reputation or character and the information is actually false.

And while we primarily have been focusing on the people who create the information that we use on the air, meaning the writers and reporters, anchors also need to be aware of these rules. The law can hold an anchor accountable for defaming someone on the air even if they only voiced the copy and did not originate it.

There are several common misconceptions concerning defamation. One is that you are not violating defamation protections if you do not use the person or group's name. That is not true if from what you have said or written it is possible for the audience to figure out who or what you are talking about. The other is that using attribution when writing or voicing a libelous or slanderous statement will absolve you of responsibility. This is also not the case. We will look at attribution later in this chapter.

False Light

This is similar to libel and slander, but is much more indirect. It means to create a false impression of someone through the improper use of audio or video.

This can happen if you use stock footage or audio in a story. This is audio or video that is available from a variety of sources on the Internet or could be material that you have simply kept from a previous story. It can

27

The Basics

also happen if you go out and shoot video or gather audio from groups of people for use in a story.

If you use this audio or video and an individual in it is recognizable and they are put in a compromising or embarrassing situation through that use, you could be in trouble.

For example, this could happen if you use that material in a story during income tax season about how many people cheat on their taxes. If a person is recognized in the audio or video that you have used in the story, it implies that they cheat on their taxes even if you do not say so or use their name in the story. When something like this happens, it is almost always done inadvertently but it does not make it any more defensible.

Plugola

A radio or television station has one thing to sell – airtime. It makes the bulk of its money by selling this airtime for commercials, sponsorships and other on-air mentions.

Plugola happens when an on-air talent, or anyone else who is responsible for what is heard or seen on the station, accepts something for that material airing. This compensation can be in the form of money, products, gifts or services.

Usually, the person or company is not aware that this is a problem when they make the offer. They are simply trying to get their message out. It is up to you to know the rules and even if tempting, refuse any type of gift connected with reporting or airing the story.

You need to evaluate the story on its own merit. If it is a good story, then it should air. If it is not, then it shouldn't . . . period. Airing or reporting a story cannot be dependent on there being any outside benefit to the station employee.

As media pros, we are not allowed to let someone, whether it is an individual or a company, influence what airs on our stations. Doing so is a violation of the Federal Communications Commission (FCC)'s sponsorship identification rule and comes with some serious penalties. You will probably lose your job and possibly your career as well, but you could also be fined as much as $10,000 and face a year in prison.

What do you do if someone asks you to commit plugola? First, you need to explain the law surrounding taking anything in consideration for

The Rules and Regulations

airing or reporting a story. Then you can offer to connect them with someone in the advertising department at the station who can help them create a commercial campaign. If they specifically want you to be involved, then that could be written into the contract. This would involve you participating either in an endorsement or testimonial commercial campaign.

An endorsement is when a celebrity or other well-known person speaks on behalf of something. They don't necessarily have to use the product. Instead they are putting their name on it. Consumers rarely make the distinction between the two. The idea is that if someone trusts or likes them, they will in turn like the product.

A testimonial is when the on-air personality relates their own personal experience and satisfaction with a product. The Federal Trade Commission, or FTC, mandates that this has to be a true story. The person has to have had actual and positive experience with the product in order to do a testimonial.

If you become part of an endorsement or testimonial project, you should be paid extra for your participation. The actual product or service can be part of the compensation for an endorsement and will absolutely be part of it in the case of a testimonial.

Some stations do not allow news reporters or anchors to be involved in endorsement or testimonial campaigns. Management can be concerned about potential damage to such individuals' credibility if a viewer or listener tries the product or service and is unhappy with it. Oddly enough, most stations have no problem with people involved in reporting and presenting weather or sports doing endorsements or testimonials.

Attribution

Attribution is the act of providing the sources for a story or for a fact or statement contained within that story. It is important to remember that attribution is not a shield for writing or reporting something that is defaming to a person or group under the conditions that we have just discussed.

We do not have first hand knowledge of everything that we report. That would require being at the scene of every news event and/or hearing everything that is said personally and that obviously cannot be done. Therefore we rely on sources. To keep the audience from thinking that

The Basics

we are the source, we need to attribute the information to the appropriate people or things.

Words and phrases that can be used in order to do this include:

- alleged, allegedly
- suspected
- accused
- reported
- according to
- as reported by

A place where this is especially important is when we are reporting on a crime story in order to avoid convicting someone of something before the courts do. Even if a person was found standing over a dead body, covered in blood, holding a knife and admitting that he killed the person, that person is still a suspected murderer, accused murderer or alleged murderer. He or she is not a murderer until the court says they are.

You also need to be very aware of attribution when dealing with quotes that you are not using on audio or video and are instead writing into your copy. You will be paraphrasing these quotes and if you do not attribute those words to the person who said them, then you make the statement a fact. And you will own that fact, meaning that if it turns out to be defaming, you and the station could be sued. We will look at this in more detail in Chapter 6.

We don't want to be skittish about reporting the facts when we write or report the news. If you are careful when writing, double-check your work, vet your sources to know that they are reliable and attribute where necessary, you should not have anything to worry about. You will be a responsible, credible, reliable and ethical reporter or writer.

Identification of Minors

This is an area where the law is very strict. Where a potential crime is involved, even if we know the identity of a person under the age of 18, we are not allowed to use it in a news story. The same rules pertain to a picture of that person. Their identities are protected.

Minor individuals can be identified if they have been charged by the court as an adult. This designation removes any protections afforded them by their age.

In non-criminal matters, a person under the age of 18 can only be identified or their picture used in a news story with the permission of their parent or guardian.

 ## Fair Use Law

Sometimes, the video or audio that you will want to use in your stories will be copyrighted. Copyrighted material cannot be used without the permission of the copyright holder. Getting that permission takes time that we generally do not have and often requires payment to obtain.

Fair Use Law allows you to use the material without getting that permission or paying the copyright holder. But its uses are very limited.

Under Fair Use, you can use copyright material if:

- You are using it for critiquing purposes. An example would be if you wanted to use a clip or audio or video from a movie that has just come out and you want to comment on it.

- You are using it for educational purposes. Fair Use allows us to use copyrighted material in a classroom setting.

- You are using it in a fleeting manner. Fleeting means that it 'comes and goes quickly'. This would apply to most news stories where we air them a few times and then they are not used anymore. Using copyrighted material in the introduction to a show where it is used every time the show airs would not be permissible under this covenant of Fair Use.

- You are using it in a parody. This is how shows like *Saturday Night Live* are able to get away with using copyrighted images, sounds and audio. It also applies to artists like 'Weird Al' Yankovic who has made a very successful career out of creating and performing parodies of songs by other well-known artists.

The Basics

 Points to Remember

- There is no excuse for inaccuracy in news writing no matter how much of a hurry you are in or what other pressures exist. You must make sure that everything you write is accurate, no matter what.
- If something is not a proven fact, it should be attributed to the source of the information.
- Defamation can apply to both people and companies and can be committed both in writing and through the spoken word.
- Defamation happens when a false statement is made about a person or company that damages or ruins its public image.
- You cannot take anything as a condition for reporting or airing a story. This includes money, products or services. Committing plugola comes with serious consequences.
- Using copyright material on the air requires the permission of the copyright holder. Fair Use Law allows you to use copyright material without permission but only in a few specific instances.

 Exercises

1. Decide if the following statements should have attribution and explain why or why not:
    - There will be no tuition increase this year.
    - The name of the new freeway is the River freeway.
    - Police arrested the murderer as he ran away from the house.
    - Income taxes are due on April 15.
    - The woman has had two previous car accidents.
    - The pills were pulled off the market after they were found to be dangerous in a new study.

The Rules and Regulations

2. Your station decides to run a report on surfing conditions every Saturday and Sunday mornings at 9am, 10am, 11am and 12pm. In the pre-recorded intro, production uses 20 seconds of a song by the Beach Boys. Is the use of this music covered by Fair Use? Why or why not?

3. Examine the following statements. Could the writer be guilty of defamation? Why or why not?

- The store at the mall sells knock-offs of expensive brands.

- The movie was his worst yet.

- The restaurant is serving portions smaller than what it advertises.

- The actor has a serious illness that may keep him from taking any other roles.

- The dog is vicious and has been known to bite other animals.

- The woman has allegedly been living at the home without paying.

- The company is not telling the truth and fires people because of their age.

> *Check the accuracy of your story and then check it again. Have more than one person who can verify it also check it. Make sure the stories line up and check their proof and accountability. Never be in a hurry to submit your piece.*
> —Gary Belzman – CBS Radio, Palm Springs, CA. Formerly KCBS-Los Angeles, Westwood One-Los Angeles

> *There is no such thing as objectivity. The only things you should strive for are fairness and balance.*
> —Bob Jimenez – former NBC correspondent and adjunct USC Journalism Professor

Ethical and Moral Newswriting

4

In this Chapter

- Professional Ethics
- Unbiased Reporting
- Fair and Balanced Reporting
- Dealing with Victims of Tragedy
- Editorializing

Increase Your Industry Vocabulary

- Balanced – Impartially presenting both sides of a story
- Editorial – A story that presents an opinion on a topical issue
- Ethics – Principles that govern a person's behavior
- Morals – A person's standards of behavior or beliefs concerning what is and is not acceptable for them to do
- RTDNA – Radio Television Digital News Association
- Unbiased – Not having or giving an opinion on a story. Being fair and not taking or promoting one side over the other

We've already examined the importance of the news stories that we select to put on the air. Now let's look at the people who do the actual work.

The media took a beating following the election of 2016. Members of the news media were accused of being dishonest and of presenting 'fake' news. While there are some in the news business who may not do an

Ethical and Moral Newswriting

honest, ethical and moral job, the majority of people in the industry take their jobs quite seriously, putting up with insane hours, travel and even go so far, in some cases, as to put their very lives on the line in order to bring stories to their listeners and viewers.

Ethical and moral newswriting and reporting has always been a major consideration in the media. The public traditionally gives immediate credibility to those of us who write, report and anchor the news. In many cases, this credibility is automatic. Over time, that credibility can grow as the person's track record and popularity grows.

Credibility is everything in this business. You lose it through unethical, inaccurate or biased writing, reporting or anchoring and you lose your career. It is really as simple as that. Once people start doubting that what you say is true, you will be ineffective as a member of the media and that will likely result in the loss of your job and a great deal of difficulty in being hired elsewhere.

In the past, it was rather rare to have a member of the media discredited and to see them leave the business. That changed in the aftermath of the 2016 election. The criticism that the media received following the election has been, for the most part, undeserved and not warranted. It was made worse by the proliferation of fake news on social media, much of which sadly is credited to the professional media when quite a bit of it appears to have been produced by people outside of the industry. It will likely take some time before the news industry fully recovers from this and it is possible that the industry will be changed forever.

There is a positive side to all of this, however. It taught the public to be a participant in the news. It forced the people who wanted to make sure they got the correct information to learn how to research and confirm stories without just accepting them as a passive viewer or listener.

At the same time, it complicated our work because there is now a sea of 'fact checkers' who are keeping an eye on our efforts like never before. And we have to deal with the inaccurate news that now is and probably always will be a part of social media.

Professional Ethics

The Radio Television Digital News Association (RTDNA) is an organization which provides visibility, advocacy, training, resources, networking and awards to electronic journalists.

The Basics

It points out that our obligation is to the public and that we must put the public's interests ahead of commercial, political and personal ones. The RTDNA suggests that our work should empower listeners and viewers to make informed decisions for themselves and not tell people what to believe or how to feel.

To aid in that effort, the RTDNA has established this set of guidelines.

Truth and accuracy above all

- The facts *should* get in the way of a good story. Journalism requires more than merely reporting remarks, claims or comments. Journalism verifies, provides relevant context, tells the rest of the story and acknowledges the absence of important additional information.

- For every story of significance, there are always more than two sides. While they may not fit into every account, responsible reporting is clear about what it omits, as well as what it includes.

- Scarce resources, deadline pressure and relentless competition do not excuse cutting corners factually or over-simplifying complex issues.

- "Trending," "going viral" or "exploding on social media" may increase urgency, but these phenomena only heighten the need for strict standards of accuracy.

- Facts change over time. Responsible reporting includes updating stories and amending archival versions to make them more accurate and to avoid misinforming those who, through search, stumble on outdated material.

- Deception in newsgathering, including surreptitious recording, conflicts with journalism's commitment to truth. Similarly, anonymity of sources deprives the audience of important, relevant information. Staging, dramatization and other alterations – even when labeled as such – can confuse or fool viewers, listeners and readers. These tactics are justified only when stories of great significance cannot be adequately told without distortion and when any creative liberties taken are clearly explained.

Ethical and Moral Newswriting

- Journalism challenges assumptions, rejects stereotypes and illuminates – even where it cannot eliminate – ignorance.

- Ethical journalism resists false dichotomies – either/or, always/never, black/white thinking – and considers a range of alternatives between the extremes.

Independence and transparency

- Editorial independence may be a more ambitious goal today than ever before. Media companies, even if not-for-profit, have commercial, competitive and other interests – both internal and external – from which the journalists they employ cannot be entirely shielded. Still, independence from influences that conflict with public interest remains an essential ideal of journalism. Transparency provides the public with the means to assess credibility and to determine who deserves trust.

- Acknowledging sponsor-provided content, commercial concerns or political relationships is essential, but transparency alone is not adequate. It does not entitle journalists to lower their standards of fairness or truth.

- Disclosure, while critical, does not justify the exclusion of perspectives and information that are important to the audience's understanding of the issues.

- Journalism's proud tradition of holding the powerful accountable provides no exception for powerful journalists or the powerful organizations that employ them. To profit from reporting on the activities of others while operating in secrecy is hypocrisy.

- Effectively explaining editorial decisions and processes does not mean making excuses. Transparency requires reflection, reconsideration and honest openness to the possibility that an action, however well intended, was wrong.

- Ethical journalism requires owning errors, correcting them promptly and giving corrections as much prominence as the error itself had.

The Basics

- Commercial endorsements are incompatible with journalism because they compromise credibility. In journalism, content is gathered, selected and produced in the best interests of viewers, listeners and readers – not in the interest of somebody who paid to have a product or position promoted and associated with a familiar face, voice or name.

- Similarly, political activity and active advocacy can undercut the real or perceived independence of those who practice journalism. Journalists do not give up the rights of citizenship, but their public exercise of those rights can call into question their impartiality.

- The acceptance of gifts or special treatment of any kind not available to the general public creates conflicts of interest and erodes independence. This does not include the access to events or areas traditionally granted to working journalists in order to facilitate their coverage. It does include "professional courtesy" admission, discounts and "freebies" provided to journalists by those who might someday be the subject of coverage. Such goods and services are often offered as enticements to report favorably on the giver or rewards for doing so; even where there is not intent, it is the reasonable perception of a justifiably suspicious public.

- Commercial and political activities, as well as the acceptance of gifts or special treatment, cause harm even when the journalists involved are "off duty" or "on their own time."

- Attribution is essential. It adds important information that helps the audience evaluate content and it acknowledges those who contribute to coverage. Using someone else's work without attribution or permission is plagiarism.

Accountability for consequences

- Journalism accepts responsibility, articulates its reasons and opens its processes to public scrutiny.

Ethical and Moral Newswriting

- Journalism provides enormous benefits to self-governing societies. In the process, it can create inconvenience, discomfort and even distress. Minimizing harm, particularly to vulnerable individuals, should be a consideration in every editorial and ethical decision.

- Responsible reporting means considering the consequences of both the newsgathering – even if the information is never made public – and of the material's potential dissemination. Certain stakeholders deserve special consideration; these include children, victims, vulnerable adults and others inexperienced with American media.

- Preserving privacy and protecting the right to a fair trial are not the primary missions of journalism; still, these critical concerns deserve consideration and to be balanced against the importance or urgency of reporting.

- The right to broadcast, publish or otherwise share information does not mean it is always right to do so. However, journalism's obligation is to pursue truth and report, not withhold it. Shying away from difficult cases is not necessarily more ethical than taking on the challenge of reporting them. Leaving tough or sensitive stories to non-journalists can be a disservice to the public.

Ethical decision-making should occur at every step of the journalistic process, including story selection, news-gathering, production, presentation and delivery. Practitioners of ethical journalism seek diverse and even opposing opinions in order to reach better conclusions that can be clearly explained and effectively defended or, where appropriate, revisited and revised.

Ethical decision-making – like writing, photography, design or anchoring – requires skills that improve with study, diligence and practice.

The RTDNA Code of Ethics does not dictate what journalists should do in every ethical predicament; rather it offers

The Basics

resources to help journalists make better ethical decisions – on and off the job – for themselves and for the communities they serve.

Retrieved from www.rtdna.org/
content/rtdna_code_of_ethics

This is not a set of rules. The RTDNA Code of Ethics is intended to give those in the news business guidelines to help them do an ethical and moral job of bringing information to the public.

Ethical decision-making is something that needs to happen at every step of the news reporting process in order to create a product that is accurate and effective.

We are faced with doing the right thing every single day of our lives, whether at work or not. And sometimes it is not easy to do. But when writing and reporting the news, we must make sure that we are doing our very best and keep in mind that what we put on the air can have a profound effect on our audience.

Unbiased Reporting

Sometimes it is hard to do, but our own personal feelings or opinions have no place in the news. There is a place for opinions. It's called an editorial and we will look at this later in the chapter. Keeping our own point of view out of stories is something that we have to always be careful to do, especially when working on stories that we might have a personal interest in or that we are especially passionate about.

That being said, it is part of our obligation to make sure that we engage in unbiased and balanced reporting.

The definition of unbiased is to show no prejudice for or against something; to be impartial. Our job is to report the facts. Just the facts. How we feel about them is irrelevant. It has no place in how we write or present the stories. It's important to keep this in mind as you write your stories. As on-air talent, you need to watch your tone of voice or inflections when you're reading the story because they can give away your true feelings even if the copy is written fairly.

40

Ethical and Moral Newswriting

Fair and Balanced Reporting

You've probably heard the phrase "there are two sides to every story". When there are two sides, it is our job to present both of them. For example, on a story about a bill that might be up for discussion in the legislature, if you were going to include what supporters have to say about it you should also include what opponents of the bill have to say as well. That's balanced reporting.

As news professionals, it is not our place to pass judgment on which side is right or wrong and your personal opinion should never play a part in how you tell the story. This decision needs to be left to our audience. Our job is simply to present the story and the facts.

It is important that you make the effort to get information from both sides, but you will not always be able to do so. You may have to go with information from only one side. The other side may not be available or may not want to give you a comment. Even if that is the case you cannot ignore that side. It is important to let your audience know that you tried to get the information. A line such as "The opposition was not available for comment" or "Our call to the supporters was not returned" or "The XYZ group did not want to make a comment for our story" will convey to your listeners or viewers that you did try to present both sides of the story.

Dealing with Victims of Tragedy

This has to be one of the hardest things to do when covering a news story. You will be dealing with a person who has just experienced probably the worst thing that has ever happened to them. There are numerous scenarios. A fire destroys a person's home, a flood ravages a town, the body of a missing child is found. And we have to talk to a person who really wants nothing to do with us. But we have a job to do and that job is to get the interview. It's an awkward and uncomfortable situation for both parties involved.

We've all heard this question asked in such situations: "How do you feel?" There probably isn't a worse question to ask. How do you think the person feels? Obviously they are hurt, devastated, numb. And often the response to the question is either a burst of tears or an angry tirade. Neither

The Basics

is usable on the air. No one wants to add to someone's pain, but by not knowing what to ask that is exactly what often happens.

So what should you ask? Years ago, I went to one of the most important seminars that I ever attended. It was on this exact topic: How to deal with victims or the families of victims. And it was eye-opening.

Understanding that we have a job to do and that we are certainly not there to inflict any additional pain on anyone, there was a panel of people who had been in a horrible situation – their children had been found murdered. They had also been the target of uneducated reporters who asked that dreaded question, "How do you feel?".

The panel talked about what would have been more appropriate questions to ask. One woman said that she was upset when the media kept referring to her daughter as "the teen" or the "16-year-old girl". She said she wanted someone to ask her about who her daughter really was. She wanted people to know that her daughter was an 'A' student, that she wanted to be a nurse, that she volunteered at a hospital and worked with children. It was amazing to see how the woman still lit up when she talked about her daughter.

I realized then that if she had been asked these questions by a reporter, not only would it have been a compelling interview, but this woman would have been happy if only for a few minutes. The reporter would have gotten something great to use in the story and would have done so without adding to this woman's pain.

Another man said he wanted to tell other parents how to protect their children. His son had been killed after his car broke down on the freeway and he had gotten out to walk to a callbox to get help. He was abducted before he made it. This was when cellphones were just coming out and they were very expensive. The man's son had been asking for one, but the man didn't see a reason to spend the money.

Now he said that if his son had that cellphone he would not have had to get out of the car and would have stayed safe. He wanted to tell parents that their children's lives were worth any price and to get their kids a cellphone.

Being able to say that to the reporter would have empowered him at a time that he felt helpless . . . and again would have been amazing audio or video to use in the story.

Dealing with a victim of a tragedy will never be a pleasant part of our jobs. But it can be a lot easier and provide a better result if we work to

Ethical and Moral Newswriting

figure out what they would like people to know and ask the right questions to allow them to do so.

Editorializing

As we've said before, our opinions do not belong in the news. But they can be included in an editorial. An editorial is a piece that is based on opinion. They are not done that often any more but used to be a daily event on many stations. Usually, editorials are done by a person on the station's management team.

The Federal Communications Commission (FCC) says that editorials have to be clearly labeled as such so that the listener or viewer is fully aware that what they are listening to is an opinion, either of the person speaking or that they are speaking on behalf of the station.

Editorials come with an FCC rule called Equal Time. In this case, if an opinion is expressed and there is an opposing side, then a representative of that other side has the right to come on and have their say. The station does not have to contact them to see if they want to take advantage of the opportunity, but has to allow them to if they ask. And the opposing view has to be aired at a time similar to the time that the original piece aired. For example, if the original editorial aired at 9am on a weekday morning, the rebuttal could not air at 2am on a Saturday. It would have to air sometime in the morning on a weekday.

Points to Remember

- Your credibility is one of your most important assets.
- Your personal opinions or biases have no place in news stories.
- Victims deserve your consideration and although you have a job to do, you need to do it with compassion.
- Editorials have to be clearly labeled as such and require stations to give those with opposing opinions equal time.
- When a story has two sides, you need to do everything you can to get information from both sides. If, for some reason, you cannot, that detail should be included in your story.

43

The Basics

Exercises

1. Each of these situations involves the need to make an ethical decision. What would you do and why choose that resolution?

- You are on deadline on a story and cannot find anyone to interview. You know your editor is not going to be happy if you write a story that does not have an interview cut in it. You have a written quote from a person involved in the story. Rather than file it without a cut, a friend at the station says he can voice the statement for you. What would you do?

- You are putting a story together and have done an interview to use in it. You did the interview on the phone and while you were doing it the person asked you to hold on for a second so they could talk to someone who had come into their office to talk about the same topic you were covering in the interview. Your recorder picked up those comments and they are good quality. They are also much more interesting than what the person said to you during the interview. Should you use the comments you recorded between the person you were interviewing and the person in their office? It would make your story better. Why or why not?

- You get to a press conference late and all the ports to plug in your microphone to get a feed from the podium are full. Ambient sound is not going to be good enough to use. A friend from another station says you can run a quick copy from her recorder after the presser is over. Once again, you need to file this story with sound. Should you record the interview from her recorder? Why or why not?

- Your story is about a bank, but the closest branch of the one in the story is five miles away and it is rush hour. You really don't have time to get there, get a shot, get back and make your deadline. There is a branch of another bank just a block away. If you don't show that bank's name, can you use it for your video? Viewers will still know it's a bank because of the signs in the windows.

2. Decide if the following sentences could be examples of editorializing or not. Explain the reason for your decisions.

- The new highway will not do anything to help traffic.

44

Ethical and Moral Newswriting

- People in the neighborhood say they are happy to see a new store moving into the area.

- It's getting dark earlier so the highway patrol is reminding you to be extra careful when driving in areas where children may be out on the streets.

- A subway through that part of town is a very bad choice by city planners.

- The mayor is used to having people follow his lead on city taxes and fees.

- Too much time and effort will be expended in trying to get the land ready for use, so the contractor has withdrawn from the project.

3. You are working on stories covering the following tragedies. Create two questions you would ask the person identified in each story. Keep in mind that you have all the details about the story itself. You are looking for some personal insight about the person or the situation.

- A man who has just returned after a brush fire to find out that his home has burned to the ground.

- A woman whose daughter has been missing for two days.

- A school principal the day that students return following a school shooting.

- A young woman who has been the victim of identity theft.

> *Remember that you're telling someone's story. You're the messenger. And most of the time you have less than 10 seconds to get a person you want to interview to trust you.*
>
> —Sid Garcia – Reporter, KABC-TV
> Los Angeles

> *Journalists should always remember that what they do is a public service. The goal should be to inform the public not to gain fame and fortune.*
>
> —John Leishser – News anchor, WCBS
> Newsradio 880, New York

45

PART III

Time to Write

Source: razorbeam.shutterstock.com

5 News Judgment – How to Pick the Right Stories

In this Chapter

- Selecting Stories
- Understanding Audience Dynamics
- Deciding on Your Lead Story

Increase Your Industry Vocabulary

- Demographics – The statistical data relating to a group or population, such as gender, age, income, education, etc.
- Lead story – The top story in your newscast based on its importance, timeliness or relevance to your audience
- News judgment – The ability to determine which stories to use in a newscast based upon importance, interest, credibility, ethics and other factors
- Psychographics – Based on demographics; the perceived attitudes, hopes, fears, desires and other psychological criteria of that group

Selecting Stories

The wire services are churning out stories 24/7, news is going on all around you, it's happening all over the world and more is being generated all the time. With that much coming at you, how do you choose what to put on the air? It's a big question and it can be overwhelming.

49

Time to Write

You need to get it right. When people hear a story they don't care about they tune out or turn off. This is exactly what you don't want them to do. We have a two-part mission when it comes to radio and TV news... Get them and keep them. Good story selection is the first step in doing that.

Let's talk first about what not to do. Every newscast can handle a certain number of stories. Selecting stories just to fill up that time is not the correct way to create a newscast. Keep in mind that airtime has a dollar value. Every minute is worth something and when you select stories to fill your newscast you want to make sure that every story is worth putting on the air and using up those valuable minutes.

So how do you select the stories? Just because a story comes down on the wire service doesn't mean that it is the right story for use on your station. As you already know, the wires service all kinds of radio and TV stations as well as newspapers. So, the stories that they produce will be appropriate for a wide variety of audiences.

Understanding Audience Dynamics

The key is to selecting the right stories and the right angles for them are to have a good sense of who your audience is. To do this you need to understand the demographics of your listeners or viewers. Demographics are the basic facts about someone, things like their gender, age, marital status, income, education level, etc.

In addition, there is something called psychographics. These are not as definite as demographics. Those are indisputable. But psychographics make assumptions about what people think, feel, fear, believe and want based on their demographics. While these will not necessarily be correct for everyone in your audience, they still will help you hone in on what type of stories your audience will be interested in.

For example, if you were selecting stories to include in your college radio station newscast, it doesn't make sense to do a story on the future of Medicare. While it would be a good story for a lot of stations, it would not be one likely to interest the majority of your listening audience. But if you selected a story about student loan rates, that story would be important to most of the people who would listen to your newscast.

Using these tools to correctly select the right stories for your newscast and for your audience is called news judgment.

50

Deciding on Your Lead Story

Once you have selected your stories, you need to pick one to be the lead or first story in your newscast. This is very important. Your listeners and viewers have come to expect that the lead story is the most important of all the stories that will be in the newscast. When we say important, we really mean the one that will most impact your audience.

Often this story is pretty obvious; at least it is on a busy news day. But, there are some days when there really is not an obvious lead. You still have to select a story to use to start the newscast. In this case, you'll need to look at the stories you have and pick the one that will be most interesting to your audience. That story will become your lead.

Points to Remember

- You need to understand your audience in order to select the right stories for your newscast.

- Demographics are the basic facts about the people in your audience; psychographics are how they feel about things.

- Your lead story should be the strongest story you have and the one that will be of most interest to your viewers or listeners.

Exercises

1. Using your college campus population as your audience, create a profile listing both demographics and psychographics.

2. Based on the demographic profile you have created for your audience, decide if the following stories should be included in your newscast and explain why. Also select one of the stories to be your lead and explain your decision.

   - A story about the price of gas going up
   - A story about a breakthrough in the treatment of dementia
   - A story about an increase in income taxes on people making more than $100,000 a year

Time to Write

- A story about a home robbery in a nearby city
- A story about a local company's pension plan going bankrupt
- A story about a new superhero movie
- A story about a new law enacted by Congress
- A story about a plane making an emergency landing in Thailand
- A story about a new giraffe being born at the local zoo
- A story about new rules about texting and driving
- A story about the mayor of a town in the next county getting married
- A story about a new drug for the treatment of diabetes
- A story about a march going on about climate change
- A story about the an actor from Hollywood's Golden Era
- A story about new rules for pre-school lunches

> *Never take anything at face value. Don't decide what angle to cover on your way to a story. There is ALWAYS a story behind the story – and it's often better than the one you planned to cover!*
>
> —Lori Kelman – News Anchor,
> KABC-AM, Los Angeles

Writing the News

6

In this Chapter

- Conversational Writing – Write Like You Talk
- Style Points
- Working with Wire Copy
- Writing from Press Releases
- Answer the Question

Increase Your Industry Vocabulary

- Acronym – An abbreviation using the first letters of the words used in the name or title of a person or organization and is pronounced as a word

- Conversational – Write like you talk. Forget the slang but also don't use words that would be perfect on a term paper but that you would never say when talking to someone face-to-face

- Copy – Another word for script

- Cut from the bottom – Editing from the bottom up in a story; useful in making a story fit in a smaller time slot than it was originally written for

- Paraphrase – Rewording of something written or spoken by someone else, especially to eliminate the statement from being in first person

- Style points – Standardization for how certain words, phrases and sentence structures are used in newswriting

Time to Write

There are a great many ways that people can get their news these days. Broadcasters are competing with information being delivered right into people's hands via smartphones and tablets or straight to their desks on their computers. That means there is even more pressure than ever to create a connection with the listener so that he or she prefers to listen or watch your newscast over getting the info elsewhere. There are a number of components that go into doing that.

A good newscast starts with good writing. The news will only sound as good as the script. But there are also a number of other things that have to be considered when writing the news. We've already discussed the legalities that need to be considered when writing and reporting the news in Chapter 3. In this chapter, we will discuss the *way* that the news is written.

Writing for radio or television is not the same as writing for a newspaper or magazine. There are several reasons why the writing style is almost the exact opposite.

First, your audience is likely not giving your newscast their full attention. If it's on the radio, they are probably driving while listening and there will be a lot of distractions. If it's on television, they may be involved in something else while the news is on such as doing homework, eating dinner or using the computer. So the way you write the stories has to be simple and the ideas in the stories have to be clear. Complicated sentences or ideas can easily confuse a listener or viewer and when they no longer know what you are talking about is when they change the channel.

With a newspaper or magazine, if you don't understand something that you just read, you can go back and read it again. Obviously that is not the case with radio or TV news. And if a listener gets confused and doesn't understand your story, then they are likely to just give up and switch the channel. So again, short, simple sentences are what we are going for.

When someone writes a story for the newspaper or for a magazine, they will write to fit a certain amount of space in the publication. With radio or TV, we write for time. But while the space in a newspaper or magazine doesn't change once the story is finished, the time during a newscast might.

That's why we need to make sure that we are able to 'cut from the bottom'. That means that the story needs to be written so if the final sentence has to be left off the story in order to hit a 'mark', such as the time we have to hit a commercial, the story will still make sense. So it's important to make sure that the most important or the newest facts on a story are in

54

the beginning of the piece and that the least important information is near the end of the story.

That's not to say that the final sentences are throw-away sentences. We should never write anything that isn't important to the story. We just need to make sure that the story will stand up and make sense without those final sentences, just in case.

Conversational Writing – Write Like You Talk

The style of presenting news has changed over the years. Years ago, the idea was that news anchors and reporters were presenting to the masses. We used words like 'everyone' and 'the people'. The attitude at times could be all-knowing or even somewhat parent-to-child.

Fortunately, that has changed. Today, we go for a much more conversational style. We want listeners and viewers to feel like we are talking directly to them and only to them. To the audience, it should seem like we were sitting next to them in the car or living room and just chatting about the events of the day.

Making this happen starts with the writing. Remember the mantra "Write Like You Talk". It really is as simple as that. If you wouldn't say something in that way, then don't write it like that.

After years of writing reports and term papers for classes as a student, you may be accustomed to using the biggest or most important words you can find and those types of words will make it into your news story. And while the words may make perfect sense and technically be the correct words, they will probably sound stilted or weird when read out loud on the radio or television.

Table 6.1 gives some examples of technically correct words and some suggested, more conversational replacements.

While in each case either word would actually be correct, which one would you normally use in conversation? When you leave campus today, you will likely go out to the parking lot, get into your vehicle and drive to your residence. But say that to someone and look at their reaction. It is much more conversational to say that you are going to get into your car and go home. And because that is the way that you would actually say it, if it's written that way, it will sound more conversational when you read it out loud.

Time to Write

Table 6.1 Conversational Word Replacement

Technically correct	Conversational replacement
Residence	House or apartment
Vehicle	Car (even if it's a truck or SUV, we most often refer to a vehicle as a car)
Citizens or residents	People
Utilize	Use
Indicated or pointed to	Showed

Style Points

When we use the word 'style' in connection with newswriting, we are referring to how the story is constructed, not the content. Many of our style points are used in order to simply make it easier, visually, to read the story and avoid making mistakes.

We are human, we are going to make mistakes on the air. It happens even to the most skilled news anchor or reporter. But if we write in a way that keeps us from having to think "what does that mean?" or "how should I say that?" when we are reading the copy, we can help keep preventable mistakes from happening.

Remember that there is a lot going on during a newscast. You may be watching the clock to make sure you hit your break on time. Someone may be giving you instructions in your headphones or earpiece. There are many occasions where you will be splitting your attention with something else even as you read the story on the air. So the easier the copy is to read, the better off you are going to be.

Here is how we handle some of these issues:

Abbreviations – These should be avoided whenever possible. It might sound silly to say don't use St. for the word Street. But St. also stands for the word saint. It might seem impossible that when reading an address someone would fail to understand that in this case, St. would mean street and not saint. But it absolutely could happen. So, we would want to write out the word Street.

It's also important to note that most of the platforms that we use to write news also time the copy as we write it. It does it by counting letters and spaces. When you use abbreviations, it can throw the timing function of the

56

Writing the News

platform off. Not by much individually, but over the course of a newscast they can add up to a couple of seconds and that can be a problem.

Here are some words that are often abbreviated, but that you should write out when they appear in news copy:

- Boulevard (Blvd.)
- Mister (Mr.)
- Mrs (Mrs.)
- Sergeant (Sgt)
- Highway (Hwy)
- Freeway (Fwy)
- Corporal (Cpl)
- the names of States
- the names of Countries

Acronyms and Initials – Acronyms are a type of abbreviation formed by the first letters of the words in the name of something and pronounced as a word. NASA is an example of an acronym. It stands for the National Aeronautics and Space Administration.

With acronyms, you have to decide if they're common enough that whoever is reading what you write will be familiar enough with them to know if they should be said as a word or as individual letters.

With NASA it's safe to think if that acronym is used in copy, that the anchor or reader will say it as a word.

But that would not necessarily be the case with CHP, which stands for California Highway Patrol. It's possible that someone seeing that in copy might say CHIP. To make sure that the initials are pronounced as separate letters, you should hyphenate them. When CHP is expressed as C-H-P, you can be assured that it will be read as three separate letters.

It or They? This might seem a bit inconsequential but in the spirit of being accurate, it is important. When speaking about an entity, such as a company or organization, the proper pronoun is **it**. When talking about the people involved with that entity, the pronoun to use is **they**.

Examples:

The police department is going to start recruiting. It says more officers are badly needed. In this case, it refers to the department.

57

More police officers would allow the department to do more public safety patrols. They would be working to make the streets safer in the downtown area. In this case, they refers to the officers.

There is an easy test for choosing the proper pronoun. If what you are talking about is human, then you would want to use they. If your subject is not human, then you should go with it.

Numbers – Numbers can cause a lot of confusion in news scripts, so we need to take extra care when using them.

The following style is designed to make numbers easier to read on the air. While we can all read numbers, with so many things going on while we are on the air, the key is to make sure the numbers are easily understood and read correctly.

The standard with numbers is that zero through ten and sometimes through twelve are written out in letters. Above that numerals can be used through the number 99. At 100, you have some options. You can stick with numerals or you can write it out as "one-hundred-thirty-one" or better, "1-hundred-31".

There are several exceptions:

- When a number starts a sentence, it should always be written out.
- Phone numbers should always be expressed as numerals.
- Addresses should always be expressed as numerals.
- Time should always be expressed as numerals.
- Years should always be expressed as numerals.

We always try to be as precise as possible when writing the news, but when it comes to numbers we don't have to be exact. When dealing with situations like acreage, death tolls and money, in most cases it's all right to round up instead of down.

For example, in a bank robbery story, if $3,791 was taken, it would be better to say "nearly 4-thousand-dollars was stolen". While it's important to include the amount in the story, it's not important to get it right down to the penny.

This can also keep a story where the figures keep changing from having to constantly be updated. A fire story or a story with death tolls are good examples of this. If you have the exact number in the story, then when it changes, the story would also need to be changed. If we round up, we

Writing the News

give ourselves a bit of leeway and only need to update the story when the number changes significantly.

Symbols – You may have noticed in the previous section that the number 4,000 was written as 4-thousand and that the dollar sign was not used. The word 'dollar' was spelled out. We try to stay away from symbols for the same reasons that we avoid using abbreviations. While we all know that $ means dollars, it is not inconceivable that with all that is going on during a live broadcast an anchor or reporter could draw a blank on its meaning when seeing it in copy. For that reason, avoid symbols and write out the word instead.

Phrases – Again using 4-thousand-dollars as an example, you'll notice that it has been hyphenated. As with all of the style points that we have been looking at, the idea is to avoid any possible confusion while reading it on the air. By hyphenating something, you alert the anchor or reporter to the fact that it is to be read all as one.

This is especially important because there is no assurance that the phrase will always end up on the same line in printed copy or on the teleprompter. Take the phrase 'over the top'. To make sense, it has to read very fluidly.

Let's see how that might look in copy. Try reading the following sentences out loud:

The event was a big success but some people said organizers went a bit over the top.

Did you take a pause after the word 'over'? If you did, your read probably sounded a bit awkward.

Here is the same sentence with the same phrase hyphenated:

The event was a big success but some people said organizers went a bit over-the-top.

The hyphen after the word 'over' lets you know that there is more to the phrase so you don't take the same pause you did in the first example.

Paraphrase – You will often see quotes included in wire copy. Often they are in first person.

It is never a good idea for an anchor or reporter to read a quote that is written in first person. When a quote is read out loud with the word 'I' in it, it makes it possible that an inattentive listener could think that the anchor or reporter is speaking their own mind rather than the words of someone else.

59

Paraphrasing a quote is pretty simple as we see in the following example. Instead of: "The woman said, 'I hate my boss and I hope I never have to see him again'", we can paraphrase it to say: "The woman said that she hates her boss and hopes she never has to see him again."

In the original example, you can easily see that a viewer or listener who is not paying attention could think the anchor is talking about his or her boss. In the rewrite, it is very clear who the woman is talking about.

Time – Just like with everything we have been doing, we need to express time in the same manner that we talk about it. We rarely say we are going anywhere at, say, 3 p.m. We would say that we are going there at 3 in the afternoon. So, that is the way we should write it. Using proper style, it would be three in the afternoon.

Use morning, afternoon and evening in your copy instead of a.m. and p.m.

Days of the week – A key function of style is to keep from confusing the audience. When we talk about the day of the week, this can be extremely important. For example, if today is Tuesday and you write a line like, " The meeting is happening Tuesday afternoon", you cause the listener or viewer to question what day of the week it actually is. When referring to days of the week, when applicable use today, tomorrow and yesterday to avoid this kind of confusion.

Working with Wire Copy

The majority of the stories we cover come down via the wire services. AP, or Associated Press, is the one most often used. It covers local, national and international news as well as sports, finance, entertainment and weather. There are others including Reuters which covers national and international news.

Within the agreement the station enters into in order to get the stories from the wire service is also a license that allows the station to use the stories on the air. That means that they actually can use the stories exactly as they come down with no edits if they wish. That's great in a pinch, but it's not the best thing to do if it can be avoided.

There are several reasons for this. The wire services don't just provide content to radio and TV stations. They also service newspapers as well and as we've already discussed the writing style between print and electronic media is quite different. So while the copy could be read on the air, it may not have the conversational style that we are looking for.

Finally, every station that subscribes to the wire services is getting the same copy. There is a possibility that another station in town might also use the story verbatim giving each of you a very similar sounding story on the air.

This doesn't mean that you have to totally rewrite the copy. That's best, but sometimes time does not allow for a complete re-write. In that case, you can do a quick clean-up of the copy. That would include replacing non-conversational words with more often used ones and cutting the length of the sentences to be shorter and more manageable.

Writing from Press Releases

Radio and TV stations get lots of press releases from groups, organizations and even companies hoping to get information about their cause, products or event on the air.

When these press releases come from companies, it's often questionable if the content is a story or really an advertisement in disguise. In Chapter 3, we discussed plugola. If you are unclear on its definition, go back and review it now.

If the press release came with any gifts or offers, then it's a better idea to simply ignore it and not use it as a basis for a story. Any gift or offer is usually an attempt to seek favor and influence the news even if it's not specifically stated that way in the press release or cover letter.

If the press release is from a group or organization and is not concerning a product, then you need to use your best news judgment to decide if it actually qualifies as a news story and whether you should work up a story from the information or not.

If you determine that you do want to use the press release as the source of information for a story, then you simply need to read the material, identify the basics such as who, what, where, when, why and how and write the story.

Take the approach that someone just came up to you and said something like "I heard that the Boy Scouts are having a big event this weekend. What's going on?" You simply need to answer the question as you write the story.

Time to Write

 ## Answer the Question

You never want to leave your audience saying, "but what about . . . ?"

One of the qualities that makes a good writer is the ability to switch places with the audience, figure out what it would want to know and include that information in the story. That can be hard because as writers we usually have a lot more information than we ultimately use in our stories. But it's important to remember that the audience is not privy to that information. All they have to go on is what we put in our stories.

Take a look at this story. What question would you have after hearing it on the air?

> The White House Correspondent's Dinner is one of the biggest social events of the year in Washington D.C. But there will be one important guest missing this year. President Donald Trump says he won't be there and he says that his White House aides won't attend either. Usually, a joke-filled speech by the commander-in-chief is one of the highlights as members of the press enjoy an evening of good nature jabs during an in-person roasting of the President. The last time a president skipped the event was in 1981.

After reading this story, what do you still want to know? That's right! **Who** was the president who skipped the dinner in 1981 and **why**? If you are going to include that final line in the story, you owe it to your audience to provide the details and not leave them hanging. Here is how the story would look with that information included:

> The White House Correspondent's Dinner is one of the biggest social events of the year in Washington D.C. But there will be one important guest missing this year. President Donald Trump says he won't be there and he says that his White House aides won't attend either. Usually, a joke-filled speech by the commander-in-chief is one of the highlights as members of the press enjoy an evening of good nature jabs during an in-person roasting of the President. The last time a president skipped the event was in 1981. At the time, then-President Ronald Reagan was recovering from being shot during an assassination attempt in March of that year.

Writing the News

It's important to re-read our stories, not just to check for mistakes but also to make sure all the details required for the stories to make sense and be complete are there. Take the approach of someone who knows nothing about the story as you re-read it. If you feel satisfied that you understand what is going on when you are through, then your story is probably complete. If you end up wondering about something, you probably should go back and provide additional detail.

Points to Remember

- Write the way you talk. Don't use words or phrases that you would not normally use in everyday conversation.

- Be conversational. Write your stories as if you were simply telling a friend what's going on.

- Style points are there to help eliminate possible mistakes so it is important to follow them.

- Tell the full story. Don't leave your audience with unanswered questions.

Exercises

1. Replace the non-conversational words (underlined) in the following sentences with ones that are more appropriate for broadcast:

- The two *vehicles* were allegedly racing on the freeway before the *collision*.

- The man *fled on foot* after he heard the alarm go off at *the place of business*.

- The two girls *expressed their excitement* when they *viewed* the puppy.

- The bank charged the man 35-dollars after *discovering* there was *a lack of funds* in his checking account.

- The student *stated* he didn't do his homework because he *suffered from a lack of time* after he got home from *his place of employment*.

- The woman was arrested at her *residence* by two members of *local law enforcement*.

63

Time to Write

- The man was confronted by two would-be robbers as he was *approaching* his *vehicle* in the parking lot.
- Students are being reminded to *adhere* to the rules when *seeking* additional time in the library.
- Firefighters were able to *extricate* the victims from the building before going in to search for an *incendiary device*.
- The work being done on the freeway is considered *imperative* to increasing overall speeds during the most *congested* hours of the day for commuters.

2. Correct the style point errors in the following sentences:

- The cost of the highway will be $200,000 and take 3 years to complete.
- The police Sgt. said the robbery was in the 3900 block of Flynn St.
- The event is set to start Fri. at 3 p.m.
- NASA is all set for the forty-fifth anniversary of the landing.
- 20 students are expected to try out for the panel.

3. Eliminate the quotes in the following sentences by paraphrasing:

- The president of the company said, "I will not be cutting any jobs during the remainder of the year."
- "I don't know exactly how the accident happened, but I did see the result", the man told the police officer.
- The woman told her son, "I will pick you up after soccer practice", before she drove off.
- The movie ended when the leading man told the girl that "I will always be there for you".

> *Most everything I know about this business, I've learned on the job. Challenge yourself to learn and evolve. Get your grammar down. Learn and remember the difference between bring and take. Learn about collective nouns. Remain passionate.*
>
> —Chris Little – News Director,
> KFI Los Angeles

Re-write and Then Re-write It Again

In this Chapter

- Pronouncers
- Proof Reading – Mistakes and Clarity
- Writing Multiple Sides

Increase Your Industry Vocabulary

- Copy – A script to either be read on the screen, on paper or on the teleprompter.
- Murphy's Law – The unwritten rule that "if something can go wrong, it will".
- News cycle – The amount of time that passes between the airing of one newscast and its next airing. Most news stations are on a 24/7 news cycle, meaning they are constantly churning out stories. Other stations might only have a couple of newscasts per hour and be on much longer news cycles.
- Pronouncer – A phonetic breakdown of a word or name to help the announcer say it correctly on the air.
- Side – A version of a story. Several sides of the same story are often written so the story can run in different news cycles and not sound repetitive.

Time to Write

Until they someday come up with avatars that present the news, and hopefully that will never happen because it will mean that a lot of us will be out of work, humans will be reading newscasts on the air. And humans make mistakes. Period.

Part of your job as a news writer is to do everything you can to minimize those mistakes. This involves certain writing techniques as we discussed in the previous chapter, but even more importantly, proof reading everything before it goes on the air. And then checking it again!

In a busy newsroom, you will sometimes be working at breakneck speeds and probably be tempted to skip this step for the sake of time. Murphy's Law says that the time you do will be the time that an error will make it on the air!

There really is no excuse for not taking the extra minute or two it needed to make sure your copy is perfect before deciding it is finished. Everyone in the newsroom is responsible for making sure that what your viewers and listeners hear and see is perfect.

Pronouncers

A neat trick that most news anchors and reporters learn how to do is to actually read ahead a few words from what you hear or see them saying. It's somewhat of a protection mechanism so that if there is an error or problem coming up, by the time they hit it, they hopefully have already figured it out or come up with a way around it. All of this, of course, happens in a matter of seconds.

It's not something that is learned or that can even be taught. It's just something that naturally happens over time for most of us.

It can be very unsettling to see a word coming up in your copy that you have no idea how to pronounce. Sometimes it's because the writer left a letter or two out, but it can also be a word that you have not seen before or is difficult to pronounce.

I recall one television news anchor in a major market who worked the early morning shift. Because the station didn't bring in a sportscaster for the shift, the anchor also did sports during his newscasts. The goalie for the local hockey team was Russian and his name was difficult to pronounce. You always knew when that name was coming up on the teleprompter. You could actually see it in the anchor's eyes as he realized he was going to have to pronounce that name again! He rarely got it right.

66

Re-write and Then Re-write It Again

Frankly, being that it was a name that came up rather often, the anchor should have practiced and practiced until it literally would have rolled off his tongue with no effort. But the point is that we often do have to deal with difficult names, places or words, many of them foreign, and that presents a problem for the on-air personalities and a responsibility for the writers.

When you're writing a story and there is a name or word that you are unfamiliar with, chances are that anyone else reading the story will also be unfamiliar with it too. That's when you need to include a pronouncer. A pronouncer gives the anchor or reporter a guideline for saying the word or name correctly. It's a phonetic representation of the word such as:

- Chechnya – CHECH'-nyah
- USS Peleliu – PEH'-leh-loo
- Qatar – KAH'-tar
- Macaroni – MAA'-kah-row-knee
- Catastrophic – cat-a-STRAW'-fik
- Colonel – KERN-all

Many of the wire services, such as the Associated Press (AP), periodically put out pronunciation guides for the names, places or words that are being regularly seen in the stories on the wires. They're updated frequently as new names and words enter the news cycle. It's a good idea to either print out these guides as they become available and keep one stashed in your desk drawer or save it to your computer. That way, you'll have it handy when you need it.

If your station doesn't subscribe to a wire service, you can always do a Google search with the phrase "how to pronounce" and then the word or name that you need to find out how to say. There are a variety of sites that will pop up with an audio pronunciation of what you are looking for. You can listen as many times as you need to be able to create the pronouncer to go in your story.

This means that you also need to be able to create pronouncers yourself. The AP uses a simple system for doing this that is designed to eliminate confusion.

Table 7.1 shows how to write vowel sounds.

Time to Write

Table 7.1 Properly Writing Vowel Sounds for Correct Pronunciation

PHONETIC	SOUND IN WORD	PRONOUNCER
a	apple	A-pull
ah	father	FAH-ther
aw	broad	brawd
ay	fate	fayt
e or eh	bed	behd
ee	tea	tee
i or ih	middle	MIH-dul
i	time	tym
oh	go	goh
oo	to	tew
ow	scout	skowt
oy	join	joyn
u	foot	fuut
uh	puff	puhf
yoo	fume	fyoom

In addition:

- Use K or S instead of the letter C (cyst = SIST, cough = KAWF)
- The letter G is always hard; use the letter J for soft G (growth = growth, gyrate = JY-rayt)
- Use CAPS to accent a syllable (Jeremy Davis = Jeremy DAY-vis).

The pronouncer should always be in parenthesis (puh-REN-thuh-seez). It's a broadcast standard that we never read anything that is in parenthesis out loud. Parenthesis aren't just used for pronouncers, but also for stage direction or anything else the writer may want to convey to the anchor or reporter as it pertains to the story.

When you put a pronouncer in your story, it should go directly after the word or phrase that it applies to. Generally, we only use the pronouncer the first time the word or phrase is used in the story. Personally, I like to have it alongside the word whenever it appears in the copy. So when I am writing a story for only myself to read on air, I will often put the pronouncer in the copy more than once just as added insurance that I won't make a mistake and mispronounce the word when it comes up a second or third time.

If there are several tricky words, it's also a good idea to put the pronunciation notes at the top of the story, so the anchor is alerted ahead of time and can practice saying the words correctly, if they do have a chance to pre-read the material.

Pronouncers aren't just used for tricky words. They can be used – and should be used – anytime that there is the possibility of a mistake being made. In the following example, a pronouncer would have really saved the day!

It happened in a story about blood donations. One of the lines was about "type O blood". I'm sure you know how to say that correctly. And I'm sure the anchor on the air at the time did too. However, it came out as "type zero blood".

It's easy to see how that could have happened if the anchor was distracted at the time and not paying 100-percent of her attention to what she was reading. Remember, when you are on the air you are doing some serious multi-tasking. There's a lot going on and a lot to keep track of, so you will be splitting your attention often, at least to some point.

You can only imagine what her audience thought when they heard her say "type zero blood". And the worst part is that it was really an easily preventable mistake simply by expressing this in copy as "type OH blood". It looks a bit strange, but that's not important. What is important is making sure that it is said correctly on the air.

Proof Reading – Mistakes and Clarity

Everyone makes mistakes. That's part of being human. And we are generally working very fast to put out a lot of stories in a short amount of time. But we should try to minimize the errors as much as possible.

There is a lot of responsibility in writing news. Not only do you have to get the facts straight, but in many cases you are writing for someone other than yourself. It's bad enough if *you* make a mistake on the air because of an error in your copy. It's worse when *someone else* is tripped up because you didn't proof read and catch your mistake.

69

Time to Write

The audience doesn't know how things work in the newsroom. Most people think that anchors write all their own stories. We know that's not true. But when someone makes a mistake on the air, that's the person who also gets the blame. It's not fair, but that's the way it is. Couple that with the fact that in very busy newsrooms, there is not always time for the anchor to pre-read their scripts and you can see how important it is that the copy be perfect before leaving your computer.

When you are reading your work, you also want to make sure that what you are trying to get across to your audience is clear. This can be a bit difficult if you already know a lot about the story. You must never assume that your listener or viewer does too.

You want to make sure that your story does these things:

- Presents the latest information
- Gives enough detail or background so that someone who knows nothing about the topic or the issue will not be lost or confused
- Has a beginning, middle and end

In the following examples, a simple error throws off the actual meaning of the story. Each is an easy fix, it it's caught before it airs.

> Governor Julie Smith spoke out the risks cops take after a Manchester police officer was wounded while chasing a robbery suspect. The police say the suspect, Jim MacPherson began shooting at Officer Hardy as soon as the officer got out of the car. They say Hardy called in MacPherson's description and the direction in which he ran after being shot.

The question here is who got shot? As written, it appears that the suspect, MacPherson, was the one who was shot. Moving a couple of words around is all it takes to make this story say what we actually want it to say:

> Governor Julie Smith spoke about the risks cops take after a Manchester police officer was wounded while chasing a robbery suspect. The police say the suspect, Jim MacPherson began shooting at Officer Hardy as soon as the officer got out

70

Re-write and Then Re-write It Again

of the car. They say Hardy called in MacPherson's description after being shot along with the information on which way Matherson ran.

Let's try another one:

> The actor revealed that he used the fate of his character in the movie to get out of a traffic ticket on a talk show with host Ben Jamison. The star said he was driving home from his parent's house when he was stopped for a traffic violation. He says the officer told him he could either follow him back to the station for booking or tell him if his character lives or dies in the next season.

What? He got off a traffic ticket while he was on the show? Of course not, but that's what it says. Once again, it's a simple fix:

> The actor revealed on a talk show with host Ben Jamison that he used the fate of his character in the movie to get out of a traffic ticket. The star said he was driving home from his parent's house when he was stopped for a traffic violation. He says the officer told him he could either follow him back to the station for booking or tell him if his character lives or dies in the next season.

Now it makes sense. It might seem like a little thing, but as news writers we are going for clarity. These were small and simple examples, but the same thing can happen with bigger and more important stories as well and cause some major misconceptions.

What makes proof reading tricky is that *you know* what you meant when you were writing the story and what your copy should say. There's a tendency to mentally fix problems as we read along and not realize the need to actually go into the copy and make a correction. When reading your copy, approach it as if you are reading it for the first time.

Writing Multiple Sides

Very few stations have only one newscast. Most have multiple casts and some even run nothing but news 24/7. Audiences tune in for various

Time to Write

periods of time from just a quick hit to being full-time news junkies. And while some stories run their course in a rather short amount of time and then are no longer used, more important ones may stay in the news cycle after cycle. So it's important to try and make sure that while the audience might hear or see the same story more than once, it's told a bit differently each time.

These different versions are called sides. Sometimes the information will change between the time you write the first, second or third sides. But often it won't. That means you will be working with the same facts over and over and still be expected to create several, slightly different sounding stories out of them.

It's not as difficult as it might sound. The key is finding a different angle in the story to use to start each side. Let's take this story about a fire at a restaurant. This would be side one:

> Firefighters were on the scene of a blaze at John's Sandwich Shop in Long Beach last night within ten minutes of it being reported, but still weren't in time to stop the fire from destroying the shop. The store's employees are being credited with thinking fast and getting customers out quickly after smoke started billowing out of an oven that was used to bake bread in the back of the store. The restaurant suffered at least 30-thousand-dollars in damage. It's not clear if the popular neighborhood hang-out will be rebuilt. Investigators are working to determine what exactly caused the fire.

The angle in this side is that firefighters got there fast, but not fast enough. Here's side two:

> Employees at John's Sandwich Shop in Long Beach are being credited with some heads-up thinking after a fire broke out last night. They moved quickly to get customers out of the building after smoke started coming out of an oven that was used to bake bread in the back of the store. Firecrews got to the scene within ten minutes of the fire being reported but were not able to save the building. Damage estimates are at least 30-thousand-dollars. It's not clear if the shop will be

72

rebuilt. An investigation is underway to figure out exactly what caused the fire.

In this version, we led with the actions of the employees.
And finally, side three:

A popular neighborhood hang-out in Long Beach has been destroyed by a fire and it's not known if it will ever re-open. The fire broke out last night in an oven at John's Sandwich Shop and quickly spread. Firefighters were on the scene within ten minutes of the fire being reported, but were unable to stop it from destroying the building. Investigators are working to find out how the fire started. The employees and customers in the shop at the time of the fire were all able to get out safely.

The focus in side three is that a popular neighborhood hang-out has been destroyed.

Each side used exactly the same information and facts. We simply rearranged them to create three distinctly different sounding stories. Now this story can be used in multiple newscasts and not sound repetitive to the viewer or listener.

Points to Remember

- You need to write for the ear and not for the eye. What you write will be read out loud so it needs to be clear and concise. Your listener or viewer cannot go back to check a fact to try to understand what you are talking about.

- Don't guess on how to pronounce difficult names or words. Find out for sure and create a pronouncer to go in your copy.

- Proof read your copy . . . and then proof read it again.

- To write multiple sides using the same facts, just change the focus of the story.

Time to Write

Exercises

1. Create pronouncers for the following words or names:
   - Los Angeles
   - Vladimir Putin
   - Africa
   - New Hampshire
   - Tabasco Sauce
   - Tequila
   - Peppermint
   - Maserati
   - Logitech
   - Tuition

2. Write two additional sides for each of these stories. Don't add any details that are not in the original versions.
   - A judge and nine lawyers listened to The Time Machines' song "Losing Myself" as a copyright trial involving a local congresswoman began. The band's music publishers are suing Katherine Smith. They allege the band's 2015 hit was copied in the soundtrack for a TV ad that aired during her successful 2014 election campaign. Smith says her campaign bought the track through a music supplier and doesn't believe they infringed on anyone's copyright.
   - It's going to be a while longer before we'll be speeding down the new freeway extension that is being built at the north end of the valley. The rains we've had recently have put construction crews way behind schedule. The freeway was supposed to be open by the end of the month. Now it looks like it will be at least the end of the summer before it's ready for drivers desperately trying to find a faster way to get where they're going. The delays have also added another 50-thousand-dollars to the cost of building the additional 25-miles of freeway.

Re-write and Then Re-write It Again

3. Each of these stories has one or more things in it that are unclear. Re-write these stories to improve their clarity.

- A three-year-old boy was taken to the hospital last night after his father accidently backed over him with the car. The child was playing in the driveway of the family's home in the Hollenbeck area of Los Angeles. The father says he didn't see him as he was heading off to a meeting at work. The little boy miraculously suffered only a few cuts and bruises.

- The local animal shelter is celebrating a very successful adoption event over this past weekend. More than 20 dogs and 15 cats found new homes. Employees say they had been at the shelter too long and were at risk of being euthanized. The two-day event was so successful that the shelter is planning to do it again next month.

> *The important thing budding broadcast journalists need to keep in mind when working on a story is to take the extra moments to make sure that you have the accurate facts. And that includes correct pronunciation of names as well as the spelling of names. When there's a question about a story detail, find out before putting the story on the air. Yes, we're always on deadline and the desire is to work fast to get the story done. But if we're wrong in any way, the story is meaningless. And you put the station, the interviewee and yourself in an awkward position. It's worth taking the extra moments to double check your facts, so when the story airs, you know you did well for the listeners, the station, the interviewee and most importantly, yourself.*
>
> —Dawn Kamber – KSBR News Director,
> Mission Viejo, CA

Types of Stories

8

In this Chapter

- Readers
- Actuality Stories
- Wraps
- To Follows
- Reax
- Question and Answer
- Man on the Street
- Kicker Stories
- Writing for Time

Increase Your Industry Vocabulary

- Actuality – A short portion of an interview – also known as a sound bite, sound, voice cut or cut. It can be audio or video

- Follows – A story that is written to be dependent on the preceding piece – it cannot be used alone because it does not contain complete information

- Kicker – An interesting or funny story, usually used to end the newscast on an 'up' note

- Man on the street – A story that uses regular people in its interviews – usually used for getting reaction to a news story or event

Types of Stories

- Question and answer – A story component made up of an interview segment in which the audience sees/hears both the interviewee and the interviewer

- Reader – A story that has no sound design or actualities in it; it is straight copy that is usually read by the anchor

- Reax – A story that is made up of reactions and is also dependent on the preceding story – it cannot be used alone because it has none of the information in it from the actual story

- Voice cut story – A story that contains one or more actualities in it

- Wrap – A recorded story in which the reporter starts and ends the piece with at least one or more actualities in between – the story is 'wrapped around' the actuality

There are numerous ways that we can do a story and a good newscast will have a mix of several different ones. Some will have actualities, some won't. Some will be read by the anchors, others will feature a reporter. This adds variety to the newscast and makes it more interesting. It can also give your audience the impression that you have a larger news staff than you do, and as we know, bigger is better.

Readers

The simplest version of a story is a reader. This is a short script that the anchor or reporter will read on the air. It can also be pre-recorded by the reporter for use later in the day.

Readers are often used when a story is just starting to develop and not very many details are available yet. They are quick to write and easy to get on the air because they don't contain any interview clips and don't require any production. Because they feature only one voice, they are generally shorter in length, meaning they can be inserted rapidly into a newscast without requiring much of a change in the other stories in the line-up.

Readers should be interspersed throughout the newscast. They should not be used to lead the newscast unless it is the only version available of a story that is really that important.

77

Time to Write

 ## Actuality Stories

These are stories that have at least one piece of an interview in them. An actuality is a small segment of an interview, either audio or video clip. It can also be called a voice cut, cut, sound, sound bite, audio or video. It is of someone either involved in the story or who knows about it such as a spokesperson. A story can contain several actualities depending on their length and the length of the story itself. We will learn more about getting and using actualities in Chapter 14.

 ## Wraps

Wraps are stories that are recorded, generally by a reporter but they can also be produced by an anchor before or after their shift for use later once they are no longer on the air.

A wrap is essentially an actuality story. The name comes from the fact that the script opens the piece, the actuality is in the middle and then there is another part of the script to end it. The actuality is 'wrapped' by the script.

Just like with the actuality story, there can be several cuts within the wrap.

Whoever writes the wrap also needs to write the anchor's lead into it. This is what the anchor will read in order to introduce the piece and the person who voiced the wrap.

 ## To Follows

As the name suggests, this is a story that is written to follow another story. It relies on the first story to provide certain details then adds others without repeating those already stated.

Here is a script that we first saw in Chapter 7:

> Firefighters were on the scene of a blaze at John's Sandwich Shop in Long Beach last night within ten minutes of it being reported, but still weren't in time to stop the fire from destroying the shop. The store's employees are being

Types of Stories

credited with thinking fast and getting customers out quickly after smoke started billowing out of an oven that was used to bake bread in the back of the store. The restaurant suffered at least 30-thousand-dollars in damage. It's not clear if the popular neighborhood hang-out will be rebuilt. Investigators are working to determine what exactly caused the fire.

A follow story to our example might read like this:

The fire department now says that it looks like the fire was a result of an electrical issue. Investigators are focusing on what appears to be an overloaded socket located near the oven where the smoke was first spotted.

You can see that on its own, this story doesn't make any sense. It needs to follow another story that has more details in it to work.

Reax

A reax story is a type of 'to follow' story. It provides reaction to a story and follows behind it. It can follow an actuality story or a wrap.

It's useful when you want to have additional insight on a story from experts or people involved in the story but don't want to include them in the original story itself. You may want to set your story up so that as the story ages and becomes less important, the reax can be dropped and the story shortened.

An example of a reax story to our example story might look like this:

Just a few blocks away, the owner and customers of City Sandwiches say they are shocked about the fire at John's. Although the two are rivals, it's a friendly competition and they say they really feel for everyone at John's. They hope the shop is rebuilt soon and in the meantime are planning to offer temporary jobs to John's employees.

This is also a handy tool to use when interviews are obtained after the original story has already been wrapped. It allows you to add the reaction interview actualities without having to re-record the wrap.

79

Question and Answer

This is another type of story that is fast and easy to get on the air. It not only adds variety but gives us another chance to get one of our reporters or anchors on the air along with someone involved in the story itself as well.

It can be used as an actuality story, a wrap, a to follow or even a reax story, depending on how it is set up.

The Q & A is just what it sounds like. It takes a recorded chunk of a question and answer session involving the reporter or anchor and uses it as an actuality.

Because it requires no real editing and a minimal amount of writing, it is another quick way to get a story on the air.

 ## Man on the Street

This is an opinion piece. The man-on-the-street interview probably should be renamed the person-on-the-street, since we can obviously interview both men and women. It's also called an MOS.

We simply send a reporter out to talk to anyone they can find and get their opinions or thoughts on a topic or a story. Usually we montage these interviews together, meaning we just edit them together one after the other. In most cases, the different speakers are not identified.

This is an effective tool to get additional sound on the air and especially with stories where there is not an expert or a newsmaker to interview. MOS pieces can be done with serious stories such as asking people what they think of a new law to softer pieces like a premiere of a movie where we interview people about the film as they leave the theater.

 ## Kicker Stories

Since most of our news is doom, gloom, death and destruction, it's nice to have a little fun every once in a while. This is where the kicker story comes in.

The kicker is usually positioned at the end of the newscast to end it on a lighter note. Usually it is simply a reader as we try to save our efforts and resources for more important stories.

The kicker can be humorous, entertainment-related, human interest or just about anything that is not of a serious nature. It provides an easy transition to sports, weather or simply a sign-off from the anchors.

Writing for Time

This is one of the hardest things to do no matter how much experience you have. We want to tell the entire story, but often we just are not given enough time to do it. It's important to know ahead of time how long your stories are supposed to be so that you can decide what details and how many actualities you will have time for.

Most stations have standards about the length of stories that must be adhered to and they can be strict about it. We talked in an earlier chapter about story count. Keeping stories shorter allows more stories to be included in the newscast.

Points to Remember

- A good newscast is made up of a variety of different forms of stories.
- A reader is the quickest way to get a story on the air.
- You can add additional details to a reporter or a recorded story by creating a 'to follow' story.
- A man-on-the-street interview is a good way to get some quick sound on the air.
- Kickers should be played at the end of the newscast.

Exercises

1. List five kinds of stories that would work for a man-on-the-street interview. For each story, create three questions that you would ask the people you interview.

2. Rewrite the following story to make it exactly 20-seconds:

   A man riding on a double decker bus on Main Boulevard allegedly robbed at least four other passengers before jumping off as the bus slowed for a stop sign Friday afternoon. Witnesses say he had what looked like a gun in his pocket as he demanded purses, wallets, cellphones and jewelry. The driver says he had no idea that anything was happening on the upper deck of his bus until he started hearing people screaming. No one was seriously hurt, but police say a number of passengers were badly shaken by what happened. Several of them were able to give investigators a description of the man, but so far no arrests have been made.

Word and syllable economy makes for a more timely, precise report, when time is costly and money is harder to find in the broadcast industry. I saw how it added up to dollars and cents with just a change of one word or two in certain times or locations in reports/scripts.

—Steve Winslow – Traffic Reporter,
WSB AM/FM, Atlanta, Georgia

Never say in two words what you can better say in one.
—Marshall Hook – Sports Anchor, WBZ-FM
98.5 The Sports Hub, Boston

Teases, Promos and Headlines

In this Chapter

- Promos
- Teases
- Headlines
- How Far is Too Far?

Increase Your Industry Vocabulary

- Headlines – Short sentences that let the audience know about several of the top stories in the upcoming newscast
- Promos – When a radio or TV station uses its own airtime to promote itself, a show, person, segment or event
- Teases – Short sentences that tell the audience about a story coming up later. A good tease gets the audience interested without giving away the story itself

For being some of the shortest things that you will ever write, promos, teases and headlines are among the most important and most difficult to write. Their job is to get people to the newscast, involved in it and through it to the end.

Time to Write

One of the hardest things about writing them is that you need to say just enough to engage the audience without giving the story away to the point that they don't have to listen to or watch it to find out what it is all about.

Promos, teases and headlines are only useful if you can make someone curious about the story itself. That's what makes them work . . . curiosity. If you write them correctly, they will pique the curiosity of the viewer or listener to the point that they will stick around to hear the actual story.

You need to be clever, crafty and sometimes . . . just a bit deceptive.

Promos

Promos are designed to get someone to the newscast. They generally combine promoting the newscast itself along with a story or two. It might also promote the anchors, reporters or someone else involved in the news.

Promos usually run in a day part away from the time of the newscast that they are promoting. That's why they need to be compelling enough to get people to remember to tune in later in the day.

A promo for the following story might go something like this:

(Promo) Coming up on tonight's news, you may have the power to save the life of a child or a pet.

(Story) It could soon be legal to break into a locked car to rescue a child or a pet. State Bill 1234 passed the Senate Judiciary Committee last week . . . and now goes on to the full Senate. Currently, only a law enforcement officer is allowed to break into a car . . . even to save a life. SB 1234 would protect anyone from being sued for damages if they believe that a child or animal is in imminent danger of injury or death. Several other states have recently passed similar laws.

Teases

Vagueness is key when writing teases, but at the same time they have to be interesting. They are most often used within the newscast to get people to stay through commercials or elements that not everyone is interested in such as business or sports.

This is one of my all-time favorites. This tease came from a Los Angeles television station early in one of its evening newscasts: "Coming up, find out why your dog's chew toy could kill you".

It came just before a commercial break followed by sports. Anyone with a dog would certainly be interested and even for those without a pet, I think it would have been hard to leave before getting the details.

As with most teases, it was not only intriguing but deceptive. The corresponding story did not come until the very end of the newscast and the payoff was, well, not really worth it. Not to say that all teases end in disappointment but they are often not all they are expected to be.

What was the gist of the story? It centered around the rawhide toys that dogs love to bury and then dig up again, often bringing the grimy, slimy thing into the house through the doggie door. The story was that if you pick it up to throw it outside and then don't wash your hands, you could end up getting sick from salmonella.

Not exactly what you were waiting for, right? I remember groaning a bit as well. But groaner or not, this tease did its job because I waited and watched all the way to the end of the newscast for the story.

Headlines

The key once again is to give just enough of the story to hook the listener or viewer. You can give more details than you did with the promo and certainly more than you did with the tease but again you don't want to give the story away.

If we use the story that we just created a promo for, the headline might be something like: "You could soon have the legal right to break a window of a hot car if it will save a life of a child or animal".

In a headline package, you are not trying to be deceptive. You are trying to give the audience a preview of a couple of the stories that will be coming up in the newscast.

The first headline will always be your lead story. Remember from Chapter 5, this is the story with the most importance or having the most impact on your audience.

85

Time to Write

Your second headline should cover a story just after the half-way point of the newscast. If all your headlined stories are early in the cast, then once they are done, your audience may think all the important stories are over, that they are done and leave.

Your final headline can be one of your lighter stories or, depending on your line up, it could possibly even be your kicker. Whatever story it covers, it should be toward the end of the cast.

Be careful not to headline and tease the same stories. Each is performing a different function and duplicating the effort can cause some confusion among your audience.

 ## How Far is Too Far?

A lot of how far you can go with a promo, tease or headline depends on your News Director and your audience.

That being said, here are some guidelines:

With promos, it's good practice not to use stories of a negative nature. These promos are likely going to be running in other types of programming, such as a television show or music on the radio show. Imagine hearing a promo during a commercial break that says "The death toll from today's earthquake goes up, details in the news at 7". What a downer!

While topically that may be something that some people are interested in and would stay tuned to get information on, it is not something that the majority of your listeners would want to hear at that point in their experience with your station. Choose something that is lighter or more entertaining.

That doesn't mean that it should necessarily be the kicker in the newscast. It just should, as a rule, stay away from doom, gloom, death and destruction.

Teases are going to be within the newscast itself or come directly before it so you can use some of the more serious stories in your line-up. But at the same time, keep in mind the purpose of the tease. It's to keep people listening over a commercial or some element that a portion of your audience is not that interested in, such as sports or business. So, it again should be something that people really want to know about.

Try to picture our previous example as a tease. "The death toll has gone up from this morning's earthquake. That's coming up when the news continues." It does work better, but is this something that people would stay around to find out more about? If you wanted to use this story, something like this might work better: "This morning's earthquake proves to be more deadly than originally thought". It's still negative, no doubt about that. But it leaves more to the imagination than the first version which gave away the fact that the upcoming story was about the death toll from the earthquake. That curiosity is what we are trying to tap into with our teases.

When it comes to the headlines, they are going to cover your biggest stories and those are probably going to be doom, gloom, death and destruction as we have previously discussed. Just like with promos and teases, their purpose is to keep the audience engaged. But since the headlines are actually part of the newscast, they can be more serious and can contain more actual information.

You still have to be careful not to actually give away the story in the headline. Again, using our earthquake example, this would be a poor choice for a headline: "The death toll from this morning's earthquake goes up to 126". With this headline, what more do you need to hear? You've gotten the latest information on the story so there is no need to continue to listen or watch. A better choice might be: "More victims of this morning's earthquake have been found".

It's also important to keep in mind that while it is possible to use the same story in all three instances, it's important to re-write it each time if you do. You want to make sure that the promo, tease and headline do not sound exactly alike.

Points to Remember

- The idea behind teases, promos and headlines is to get viewers or listeners to stick around to hear the story.

- You want to be careful not to give the story away. If you do, there is no reason for people to wait to hear the entire story.

- It is best to stay away from extremely negative stories for promos.

Time to Write

- While you need to be creative when writing teases, promos and headlines, you still need to stick to the facts and avoid sensationalizing or being over-dramatic.

Exercises

1. Create a promo, tease and headline for the following stories. Each one should increase in its intensity and detail:

> Millions of people took their message about climate change and other scientific issues to the streets across the country today. The March for Science was a show of support for fact-based research and environmental protection at a time when federal funding for researching climate change and other science-related initiatives is under threat. They carried signs that read "There is no Planet B", "The Earth does not belong to man" and "The Good Thing about Science is that it's True whether You Believe it or Not!" More than 500 marches took place across the country. They took place on the 47th anniversary of the first Earth Day.

> A year ago, Pokémon Go was all the rage. People were searching for the cute little creatures everywhere . . . especially in parks. The company behind Pokémon Go is Candy Lab Incorporated in Irvine, California. It's now suing Milwaukee County over a law it passed a few months ago over the huge crowds that Pokémon Go attracted to one of its parks. The county said the Pokémon hunters repeatedly left the park a mess with trash and debris and kept other people from enjoying the park. The county also had to cover the huge cost of cleaning the park up. Candy Lab is now developing another augmented-reality game called Texas Rope 'Em! The variation of the card game Texas Hold 'Em is currently being tested in several cities including Milwaukee, Austin and London.

> *Go into broadcasting because you love it. Don't go into it looking for money. Always do what you can to better your position, but look for other revenue streams that can help you get ahead in life.*
>
> —Randy Fuller – News Writer and Anchor,
> NBC Radio News, Los Angeles

Enterprising Stories

In this Chapter

- Finding Ideas
- Sourcing the Story
- Relevance to the Audience

Increase Your Industry Vocabulary

- Enterprise story – A story not based on wire copy or a press release. The reporter comes up with the topic on their own
- Green light – To give the go ahead for something to happen or be done

Most of us in the news are always coming up with ideas for stories that we would like to do. A lot of the time, though, we don't have a chance to do them. When we do it is called enterprising.

With an enterprised story, you are in charge. You come up with the idea, do the interviews, write the copy and voice the piece. You may even do the production on it, if you are skilled enough and there are no union restrictions. It is truly your own creation.

If your station doesn't suggest enterprising stories, you can always ask if you can do stories on your own. You might be required to get approval on the topics before you start. Sometimes, you will be able to get some time off from your regular assignment to work on enterprise pieces. More

Enterprising Stories

often, though, you will be told that it's fine if you want to do one, but it will be on your own time. In either case, you are demonstrating that you want to be an active part of the news process at your station and that you are able to think out of the box. Both of these are things that can help you to advance in the field.

Whenever I've gotten the chance to create an enterprise piece, I've gone ahead and done it. Enterprising lets you get a story out there that you feel the listeners and viewers should or would want to hear or see. It might center around your passion. It might focus on something that happened to you or that you witnessed. It's odd, but these stories often seem to write themselves. It might be because when you come up with an idea and get to carry it out, you simply are more interested and excited about the project. Many of my awards have come from these pieces.

In any case, enterprising can be fun.

Finding Ideas

Ideas are all around you. They can come from just about anywhere.

If you see something and wonder what that is all about, it might work as the topic of an enterprise piece. If something happens to you that teaches you a lesson, you might be able to turn it into one.

I was once driving through a town in Southern California and saw a whole lot of life-sized statues of sheep on the center medians of some of its major streets. Each one was painted in wild colors and designs. What were they doing there? Who put them there? And why? I had no idea and if I didn't, then it makes sense that other people didn't either. So when I got to the station, I started making calls and a really fun story developed.

It turned out the sheep had been painted by local artists and were going to be sold at auction to benefit a community effort. They had been put on the center medians so people would see them and hopefully participate in the auction to own one for themselves.

Another enterprise piece came out of something that actually happened to me. A chain of gas stations was promoting a small device that you could put on your keychain to speed up the process of buying gasoline. The device had the information from your gas station account on it and you would simply wave it at a logo on the gas pump and be able to pay for your purchase.

91

Time to Write

Mine suddenly stopped working and I called the company. After giving the representative the code on the device, I was suddenly switched over to the fraud department! Turns out I had a device on my keychain that had been stolen. In talking with the representative, we determined that when I gave my car keys to the attendant at a car wash, that person must have switched my device with one that had been stolen and deactivated. Since they all looked alike, no one would notice till they tried to buy gas and found the device didn't work, which is exactly what had happened to me. And sure enough, there were purchases on my account that I had not made. They deactivated my original device immediately and sent me out a brand new one after a stern lecture on not leaving the device on my keychain when giving it to someone for any type of car service.

I got to thinking that if this could happen to me, it could happen to people in my audience. I called the company back, did an interview with the head of their fraud department and did the story. We got a great response from the audience when it aired. Some said it had happened to them; others were thankful that we had made them aware of the situation so it would not happen to them.

The story allowed us to really connect with our audience and I felt good for doing something that would help the community.

If you want to enterprise stories, just keep your eyes and ears open. You'll find plenty of great ideas.

Sourcing the Story

Unlike stories that come down the wire services or that you work up from a press release, with an enterprise story you have to figure out how to do everything yourself. This will take a little work.

The key will be your interview or interviews. You need to find experts to talk on the subject or you might want to go with individuals who have been or will be involved. Although an enterprise story is your creation, you still need to have voices other than your own in the piece.

You can do a lot of this background work on the Internet. You may be able to find websites that deal with your topic and find someone to talk with through the contacts page. You might find articles that will give you additional information and could lead you to someone to interview. You may also find websites that deal with your topic. Make sure, though, that if you

Enterprising Stories

use any material from a website, you include proper documentation in your story. We discussed attribution in Chapter 3.

Any time that we use sound, there are a few things to consider. First is not to use sound for the sake of sound. Make sure that any cut you include in your story actually contains details that help to tell the story. Just don't drop in an actuality because you know you need one. Consider using more than one cut or cuts from different people. You might also consider using sound from the scene to help people picture what is going on. This is called ambient or nat (natural) sound. We'll look more at using sound in Chapter 16.

Relevance to the Audience

Unless you have very different interests or experiences from those of your audience, pretty much any topic will be appropriate for an enterprise piece. With such a piece, you are not so much reporting news as you are covering human interest.

But you still need to consider audience demographics. They may not be the same as your own demographics and that can make your enterprise idea not relevant. While a thoughtful piece on selecting a proper home for aging parents might be an excellent idea, if your audience is very young, they will likely be unable to relate. As with any choice we make when selecting stories, writing them or reporting on them, we need to remember who we are talking to and what they're interested in.

Points to Remember

- You may have to do enterprise stories on your own time, but they are worth doing. They show that you want to go above and beyond and that can help your job security and job growth. They also give you a chance to work on a story you are really interested in.

- When you work on an enterprise story, you have to make all the decisions and construct the story from scratch.

- There are ideas for enterprise pieces all around you. Look at things you are interested in, experiences you have or things you are curious about as possible topics.

Time to Write

Exercises

1. Create a list of five stories in your community that you could use for an enterprise story. Explain why each story would be interesting to your audience. Detail what experts you would interview for your story. What pictures or video would you want to shoot in support of your story?

2. Write a proposal for an enterprise story concerning something on your school campus. Create this with the purpose of convincing your Program Director to give you the green light to proceed with the story. You will want to summarize your idea for the story, list the experts you would interview and explain why your audience would be interested in your story.

> *You're more likely to sustain success if you can combine your talents with your passion. Be willing to do what nobody else will so you make yourself indispensable . . . it's how I have survived endless rounds of layoffs! Diversify your skill sets as an insurance policy and always have contingency plans in mind. One can never become complacent in this business.*
>
> —Desmond Shaw – Airborne Reporter,
> CBS Radio and TV, Los Angeles

> *First, devote your career to being a credible messenger, not to aspiring to become a star entertainer. And secondly, for heaven's sake, learn the difference between 'fact reporting', 'investigative reporting', 'analysis', and 'commentary'. Focus on one and only one of those, and be the best at it; don't try to combine them, no matter how tempting the money and glory may be. Remember that just because a media outlet uses the word 'news' in their name doesn't mean they are all about real unbiased journalism.*
>
> —Ed Reed Walker – Retired Reporter, Anchor,
> Air Personality and Program Director
> with KSEL (Lubbock), KLBJ
> (Austin), KAYI (Tulsa), KBST
> (San Marcos, TX)

Creating Series or Multi-part Stories

In this Chapter

- Purpose and Benefits
- Outlining the Story
- Developing the Story
- Finding Experts to Interview
- Formatting the Story
- Recapping the Previous Segment

Increase Your Industry Vocabulary

- Anchor tag – An additional, short piece of copy that is read by the anchor. It usually contains information that may change (such as an acreage count) or adds additional information to the story. Because the tag is read live, it can be changed at any time to update the original story
- Story board – A sequence of drawings or pictures that show the progression of a story
- Story count – The number of stories contained in the newscast. Some stations will shorten stories to make sure they hit a certain story count

Purpose and Benefits

Story count is important on commercial radio and television stations. It's not as important but still matters on non-commercial or public stations.

Time to Write

Story count is the number of stories in any given newscast. There is always somewhat of a battle between the number of stories we can fit in the cast and the length of those stories.

Some stories simply need more time than others. In those cases, we can sometimes create multi-part stories or series. These give us more time to develop the topics or to present a variety of different angles within the story.

There is another benefit to the multi-part story. It's a way of getting listeners or viewers to return to the station to hear each additional segment, day after day. It works much the same as a mini-series on television. If we can get someone hooked on the series, they will come back because they are invested and curious to find out what comes next.

The topic of a series can be serious or it can be more lighthearted. Essentially, it can be anything that lends itself to the multi-part approach, meaning there is more to the story than can really be fully told in the traditional one-part story approach.

Outlining the Story

Multi-part stories are similar to the 'to follow' stories that we looked at in Chapter 8, except that they are able to stand on their own. If you recall, the 'to follow' stories were totally dependent on the connecting story in order to make sense. In the case of the multi-part story, each episode or installment has enough information from the preceding part that the audience can understand it even if they did not hear the series from the beginning.

One of the most important steps you can take when creating a multi-part story or series is to outline it so you know where each episode will go. This is how you get started. Because you do not have to include everything in one episode, you can add a lot more detail than you normally get to with a single story.

You start with your topic. Then you create a 'verbal storyboard' for your series.

Let's take the simple topic of nuisance dog barking. It might not seem like there is a lot you can do with this topic. But once you start brainstorming, the subtopics start to fall into place. Consider all the things that a person would want to know about dogs that bark all the time. Think about it from a dog owner's point of view and also from the standpoint of the people who live close to the barking dog.

96

Your storyboard might look like this:

- Part 1 – Introduction to the problem
- Part 2 – Why dogs bark
- Part 3 – Current laws dealing with barking dogs
- Part 4 – What can happen if a dog barks too much and is reported
- Part 5 – Remedies for dogs that bark excessively

Developing the Story

Now that you have an idea of how the various parts of the story will go, you need to develop each one and determine what experts you can interview for the piece.

- Part 1 – Introduction to the problem
  - What is it like to live near a dog that never stops barking?
  - How big a problem is this? (Look for local statistics on the number of barking dogs animal control deals with each year.)
- Part 2 – Why dogs bark
  - What causes a dog to bark excessively?
  - Are some breeds more apt to bark than other breeds?
- Part 3 – Current laws dealing with barking dogs
  - What laws are on the books about dog barking?
  - How much barking constitutes too much?
- Part 4 – What can happen if a dog barks too much and is reported to authorities
  - Steps that animal control can take
  - Steps the dog's owner can take
- Part 5 – Remedies for dogs that bark excessively
  - Different training methods that can help a dog stop excessive barking
  - Other things that a dog owner can do to keep the dog from barking

Time to Write

 Finding Expert Interviews

Now that you have your story outlined with your subtopics, the next step is to decide who to interview for each segment. You need to find people who would have information or expertise within each area of your series.

- Part 1 – Introduction to the problem
    - What is it like to live near a dog that never stops barking?
    - How big a problem is this? (Look for local statistics on the number of barking dogs animal control deals with each year.)
    - **Interview – someone within animal control**
- Part 2 – Why dogs bark
    - What causes a dog to bark excessively?
    - Are some breeds more apt to bark than other breeds?
    - **Interview – a veterinarian or dog training expert**
- Part 3 – Current laws dealing with barking dogs
    - What laws are on the books about dog barking?
    - How much barking constitutes too much?
    - **Interview – more with your animal control contact**
- Part 4 – What can happen if a dog barks too much and is reported to authorities
    - Steps that animal control can take
    - Steps the dog's owner can take
    - **Interview – more with your animal control contact or an attorney who specializes in animal matters**
- Part 5 – Remedies for dogs that bark excessively
    - Different training methods that can help a dog stop excessive barking
    - Other things that a dog owner can do to keep the dog from barking
    - **Interview – more from your dog training expert**

Formatting the Story

Setting up the segments of a series is different from the way we format a regular one-piece story.

We want to remind people that what they are hearing or watching is a series or multi-episode piece. We do this in the intro and at the end of each installment. We also need to make sure that each piece makes sense on its own so we don't lose listeners or viewers who missed the previous parts.

Keeping with our dog barking example, the lead to the first episode might look something like this:

> Dogs bark. That's normal. But some dogs bark a lot more than others and that can be tough if the barking dog lives next door. KXYZ's Tammy Trujillo looks at the problem . . . and solutions . . . in the first of our five-part series on Noisy Dogs.

This intro to part one of our series almost sounds like a promo and in a way it is. The normal intros to wraps that we looked at in Chapter 8 simply introduced the reporter and created a jumping off point for the story. In the intro to the multi-part story, we need to let the audience know what they can expect from the series itself. It's the first of several efforts that we will write to try and get people invested to the point that they will make an effort to hear every episode.

The outcue for the piece will also be similar to a promo. This time it will be for the next installment of the series. Here is an example:

> Dogs rarely bark for no reason. In part two of our series, Noisy Dogs, coming up tomorrow at this same time (or whenever you have it scheduled), we'll look at the reasons a dog might bark non-stop. I'm Tammy Trujillo, KXYZ News.

Recapping the Previous Segment

We hope that people will hear all of the pieces of our multi-part story, but that doesn't always happen. We want to make sure that even if someone has missed the previous installment, the piece they are currently hearing will still make sense.

Time to Write

We do this by quickly recapping the information in the previous segment in the lead to the next part of the story.

Here is how this might work:

> If you live next door to a dog, you obviously have heard it barking from time to time. But some dogs never seem to stop and that can be unbearable. In part two of our series, Noisy Dogs, KXYZ's Tammy Trujillo looks at the reasons some dogs bark . . . and bark . . . and bark.

We didn't give a lot of detail from the first part, but we did cover briefly what it was about. We also let the listener know that they are hearing part of a multi-part story.

The outcue for part two would again promo the upcoming installment of our series. It might sound like this:

> No matter what the reason is for a dog barking non-stop, there are laws to protect neighbors who just want peace and quiet. We'll take a look at where authorities stand on the problem tomorrow at this same time (or whenever you have it scheduled) in part three of our series, Noisy Dogs. I'm Tammy Trujillo for KXYZ News.

You would continue this pattern of linking your one segment with another and then promoting the next segment in the outcue until your series is finished. The outcue to your final segment would simply be a standard station outcue, the same as you would use in any regular single-segment story.

Multi-part stories also provide an opportunity to drive traffic to the station's website or social media. The station could post segments of the series that have already aired and you could add a line in your outcue directing your viewers or listeners to the site to hear what they have missed. Any effort to push traffic to the station's Internet effort is usually a winning idea with management.

Points to Remember

- You start a series by outlining the various segments. It will help you determine how you will break down the story over the various episodes.

Creating Series or Multi-part Stories

- A segment requires that you have several experts to use for the interviews that will generate your actualities.

- You want to do a quick recap of the previous segment in the lead to each segment and promo the next segment in each lock out.

- Multi-part stories can be used as a vehicle to push traffic to the station's website or social media.

Exercises

1. Create a verbal storyboard for the following story. Plan on making your story a five-part series.

> The first in a network of electric vehicle charging stations is now on line in North Park. Under the 22-million-dollar "Charge Up" program, more than one-thousand stations across the state will be involved over the next year. The company says that the adoption of electric vehicles is a very important part for helping the state meet its environmental goals. And it's especially important to cities along heavily traveled transit corridors like the ones through North Park where people are breathing smog every day. The pilot program will install charging stations in places where drivers are expected to park for longer than four hours – like school campuses and some workplaces. If the pilot program proves successful, North Park Utility plans to get a bigger 355-million-dollar program approved to expand the network to 30-thousand stations.

2. Develop your story from the storyboard you have developed. How would you expand each of the topics in the five parts? Who would you interview?

> *My career was a dream come true in every way. It was another era where good journalism was part of everyone's life. Truth and accuracy were assumed. I was writing the first draft of history. If you have a passion for journalism, go for it. It's hard work but nothing is more rewarding.*
>
> —Linda Deutsch – Special Correspondent
> 1967–2015 at The Associated Press

Public Affairs and Public Service Announcements

12

In this Chapter

- FCC Requirements
- The Public File
- Working with Ascertained Issues
- Finding Interesting Topics and Guests
- Preparing for the Interview
- Post-show Responsibilities
- Public Service Announcements
- The Quarterly Report

Increase Your Industry Vocabulary

- Ascertained issues – Topics and issues that are of concern and importance to the community
- PSA – Public Service Announcement – an on-air announcement available for free to non-profit organizations to promote their cause, events or groups
- Public affairs programming – Talk shows addressing the station's ascertained issues. The FCC requires that one hour per week be dedicated to public affairs

Public Affairs and PSAs

- Public File – Also known as the public inspection file. It's the station's collection of official documents that the FCC requires all radio and television stations to maintain
- Quarterly Report – A report that is done at the end of every quarter reflecting the station's news, public affairs, political and other programming as it pertains to broadcasting in the public interest

One of the main tenets of a radio or television station's FCC license is the vow to broadcast in the public interest. One of the main ways this is done is through public affairs shows and Public Service Announcements (PSAs).

Depending on the size of the station, these duties often fall to the New Director of the station. Very few stations have an actual Public Affairs Director these days.

Public affairs shows can be a lot of fun to do. They give you a chance to go in-depth on topics of public interest and do interviews of much longer lengths than for the usual news story.

FCC Requirements

Over the years, the FCC has reduced or eliminated many of its requirements for a station to retain its license to broadcast. The public affairs commitment still exists.

Tune into most radio or TV stations early on a Sunday morning and you will likely hear a public affairs show. Per FCC rules, stations are required to run one hour per week of public affairs. This can be broken up into two 30-minute segments or be a solid hour. It's up to the individual station to decide which way it wants to fulfill this commitment.

Public affairs shows must be sponsor-free. Because public affairs shows cannot contain commercials, stations tend to run them at times when it is harder to sell airtime and when the value of those spots are generally lower than at other times of the day. That is why most stations air their shows early on Sunday mornings. Some stations will also put the shows on late Sunday nights.

Because public affairs shows are an FCC requirement, there is documentation required and this must be contained in the station's Public File.

103

Time to Write

The Public File

The Public File is required of every FCC-licensed radio and TV station in the country, no matter how small it is or where it's located. This includes college radio stations.

The FCC is very serious about a station's Public File. Failure to include the proper documentation or incomplete documentation of the station's public affairs efforts, among other things, can result in serious fines.

There are a great many things that must be included in the Public File. From a news standpoint, the only ones that we are concerned with are the public affairs show summaries and the Quarterly Report.

If you are also handling PSAs, you may include a quarterly list of the groups featured in the PSAs that have run on the station. This is not an FCC requirement but some stations still do it in an effort to simply provide additional evidence of their involvement in the community and providing non-profit groups with access to their airwaves.

As of March 2018, the FCC has started requiring a station's Public Files to be posted online. Your station may already have a link from its website to a place for its Public File on the FCC website. Until this date, the Public File had to be kept in the station's city of license, whether that be at the station itself or somewhere else in the city. Traditionally, that would be the city library if the physical location of the station was not in its city of license.

Working with Ascertained Issues

There are a variety of topics that must be addressed by your station's public affairs show. These are called ascertained issues. They are the issues that your audience is most concerned with. Often they remain the same year to year, but sometimes will change as they reflect what is going on in your community or in the country.

Common ascertained issues include: health, traffic, the economy, education, jobs, homelessness, the environment, housing, crime and drug use.

Finding Interesting Topics and Guests

There truly is a never-ending supply of guests for a public affairs show and you will find that most people are very happy and even honored to be invited to be a guest.

News stories are an excellent source. Since news pulls from your local community, there are a lot of stories that can be expanded to become a topic for your public affairs show. A story about new lanes being built on a local freeway could easily turn into a show on traffic problems in the area and solutions that are in the works. A story about the first instances of the flu season could be turned into a show about the flu including things like how scientists determine which strains should go into the yearly vaccine, why the flu shows up each year and what to do if you get it.

Your radio or TV station probably gets a lot of press releases. Looking through these periodically can give you ideas and contacts for shows. Press releases are sent by groups or organizations looking for publicity, so the people involved will generally be very interested in being a guest on your show.

Every community has charities that are always trying to raise money for their various causes. A quick phone call or visit to their websites will likely give you a calendar of their events. Follow that up with a phone call and you will likely be able to put together a show that focuses on the group and what it does and then features the event, possibly promoting and giving your audience an opportunity to participate.

Nearly everyone is on social media these days. So are a lot of groups. Many times an issue that is trending can be turned into a show. You need to do a little research and then determine who your guests should be but you will end up with a show that is top-of-mind with much of your audience.

Just about any topic can work as a subject for your public affairs show so your inspiration can come from just about anywhere.

Preparing for the Interview

You'll need to call and schedule your interview. Public affairs shows can be done live in the studio, but because of the time of day that they are usually scheduled to air, most of the time they are pre-recorded.

Because the person you will be interviewing is probably not used to being interviewed, you will often be asked to send them the questions you plan to ask in advance. It is not a good idea to do this. There are a number of reasons. First, you don't want your guest to practice the answers or worse yet, to write them out so they can read them back to you during the show. In both cases, the answers are going to sound 'canned' and fake.

You also don't want to get locked into a list. A good interviewer will go into an interview knowing pretty much want they want to ask, but also able to ask questions prompted by answers to their questions. You want to let the interview flow like a normal conversation.

Instead, tell your guest that you will go over a quick outline of how you see the show progressing before you begin, but that you find that more people will listen if the show is more of a conversation than a strict question and answer session.

As for your preparation, how much you do is up to your own style. I actually do very little preparation. I don't want to know so much that I don't ask the questions my audience would ask if they were sitting in my chair. When it comes to interviews, we always have to remember that our audience may know little or nothing about our topic, so we have to ask the basic questions for them before we ask the more advanced ones. I want to discover *with* my audience. This approach leads to doing an interview that will satisfy your listeners and keep them engaged.

Post-show Responsibilities

It's a good idea for your public affairs show to have a presence on social media. Even though per FCC regulations no advertising can be sold on your show so ratings are not an issue, that doesn't mean you shouldn't be promoting in an effort to create a loyal listenership for your show.

Create social media accounts under the name of your show. Then each week, post a quick notice about who the guest will be on your next show and a little synopsis of what you will be talking about. If you took a picture with your guest you can use add that or post a link to the group's website. You will not only add to your audience for the show, but you will also solidify a good relationship with your guest which can come in handy for future interviews.

Most stations will not allow you to post the show itself online until after it airs. Be prepared for your guests to ask you for a copy of it or a link to where they can download it. Check with your station to make sure that providing a copy through any method is within the company guidelines.

You will also need to create a summary of the show. There is no specific form for this, even though it is an FCC requirement. You can design your own format as long as it includes certain pieces of information:

KXYZ (name of show)

SHOW #:

NAME:

WEBSITE:

HOST:

RECORDING DATE:

AIR DATE:

DURATION:

ISSUES:

This summary needs to be included in the station's Public File.

Public Service Announcements

Airing PSAs or Public Service Announcements is no longer required by the FCC but stations still often put them on the air. PSAs do not have to be documented, but some stations still do that just to show the FCC their commitment to the communities that they serve.

Here is an example of a 30-second PSA for an agency that helps people during disasters:

> Thousands of families affected by disasters urgently need support. You can help Your County Partners provide warm meals, shelter and hope to families when they need it most. Please

Time to Write

donate today to Your County Partners so they can be ready to help people in your own community. Go to Your County Partners-dot-com or call 1–800–123–4567 today. Your support is critical. We can't do it without you. Thank you!

The Quarterly Report

This document is a culmination of the weekly summaries that are prepared for each public affairs show that airs. It is not as detailed as the individual show reports. Again, there is no real FCC format for this document. Most stations simply make a list of air dates and topics. Many also include the show reports in order to provide additional information in case the FCC would like to see it.

The Quarterly Report is due in the station's Public File on the 10th of the month following each quarter.

- January–March shows – Quarterly Report must be in the File by April 10
- April–June shows – Quarterly Report must be in the File by July 10
- July–September shows – Quarterly Report must be in the File by October 10
- October–December shows – Quarterly Report must be in the File by January 10

Points to Remember

- Radio and TV stations are required to provide one hour of public affairs programming each week.
- The shows are based on the ascertained issues as determined by the individual station.
- Each show should generate a report which can be used to create the Quarterly Report.
- The Quarterly Report needs to be kept in the station's Public File.

108

- Stations are no longer required to run Public Service Announcements (PSAs) but the majority of stations still run them as an added commitment to broadcast in the public good.

Exercises

1. Suggest a topic and guest for the following ascertained issues:
   - Health
   - Traffic
   - Economy
   - Employment
   - Housing
   - Homelessness
   - Crime
   - Drug Use Prevention
   - Environment
   - Education

2. Select a non-profit group in your area. Use information from its website to create a 30-second PSA for the organization. Turn in your original information with your PSA.

> *Remember to be a professional broadcaster. You must be flexible and be ready for whatever may come your way. And let the truth come to the forefront because it always does.*
>
> —Jim Hall – Former broadcaster at
> KHJ, KRLA, KAVR, KFOX,
> KCIN – Los Angeles
> Retired Associate Professor of Broadcasting
> and Communications, USC

Other Types of News

13

In this Chapter

- Sports
- Business
- Traffic
- Weather

Increasing Your Industry Vocabulary

- Dow Jones – A group of significant stocks
- NASDAQ (NAHZ-DAK) – The second largest stock exchange in the world
- New York Stock Exchange (NYSE) – The largest stock exchange in the world
- S-and-P 500 – A group of 500 large companies that have common stock listed on the NYSE or NASDAQ
- Sig Alert – A traffic term that applies to any unplanned event that will tie up one or more lanes on a major route for more than 30 minutes
- Stock Market – A collection of markets and exchanges where stocks, bonds and other securities are exchanged or traded

Sports, business, traffic and weather . . . they sometimes scare the life out of broadcasting students when they have to include them in their newscasts. And in a way, rightly so. With respect to sports and business, members of

Other Types of News

your audience likely know more about these topics than you do. And in the cases of weather and traffic, they may have a front row seat to what is really going on.

But if your station requires these topics to be included in your newscasts, you have no choice. So what do you do? There's something called the KISS method. Keep it simple, stupid (sorry, no insult intended). But it's key to dealing with these four areas.

If you know sports, you're in luck. Adding a few lines about sports or even creating a complete sportscast will be easy for you. Your biggest problem will probably be wanting to add too much, getting too far into statistics or running out of time.

If you don't follow sports, then keep the KISS method in mind. We will look at the basic information that you need. Stick to that, don't get too fancy and you will do all right.

Sports

There are a few basic guidelines to follow. Keep in mind that your station may want something different, but aside from that you basically want to focus on your local pro teams in the major sports: baseball, basketball, football, hockey and soccer. If other sports such as golf or tennis are involved in a major tournament like the Masters in golf or tennis's Wimbledon and names a winner, you should add that information if you have the time.

In some markets, college and even high school sports, especially football and basketball, are big deals, so they would be included as well and perhaps even lead your sports effort. A quick conversation with your Program or News Director or a check of the front page of the sports section of your local newspaper will help you get a perspective on the hierarchy of sports in your area.

Just like with the news, you will be able to find a lot of source copy on the wire services. Audio and video will also be available.

The members of the audience who follow sports, FOLLOW sports. They know what is going on. This means that you need to make sure you know certain things:

- The correct names of the teams. This can sometimes be tricky. For example, the Colorado Rockies play baseball, while the Colorado Avalanche play hockey. You do not want to get them reversed.

Time to Write

- How the teams score and how the game is broken up:

  1. Baseball is scored in runs. The game is played in innings. Nine innings makes a game unless the game is tied at the end and then it goes into extra innings.

  2. Basketball is scored in points and is played in four quarters or two halves. There is a break at half-time. If the game is tied at the end of the fourth quarter, it goes into overtime. The game can go into several overtimes until the winner is decided.

  3. Hockey is scored in goals and is played in three periods. If the game is tied at the end of the third period, the game then goes into a five-minute overtime. If it's still tied, the game goes to a shoot out. If neither team takes a lead, the game goes to sudden death and the game can still end in a tie. (Don't worry, we'll talk about how to handle this shortly.)

  4. Football is also scored in goals and is played in four quarters or two halves. There is a half-time in between quarters two and three. If the game is tied at the end of the fourth quarter, one overtime is played and if neither team goes ahead, the game can end in a tie.

  5. Soccer is scored in goals and lasts 90 minutes. At the end of that time, the team with the most goals wins. If there is a tie, the winner is decided either by an extra 30 minutes of play or a penalty shoot-out.

  6. Tennis is scored in points and played in sets. Play continues until one player wins the best of three sets or five sets, depending on the tournament.

  7. Golf is played in holes. Usually there are 18 holes to a game. The player who has the best score wins (roughly based on how many attempts it took them to get the ball into each hole). That's called 'over-par' or 'under par'.

Do you really need to know all of this? The answer is no. But you do need to know enough to make sense of what you will see on the wires and to say it properly. Here are some examples for each sport:

- Baseball: "The Dodgers beat the Braves 5 to 4" or "The Mets were 6–3 winners over the Reds in 10 innings" (indicates the game went into extra innings).

112

Other Types of News

- Basketball: "The Clippers edged out the Bulls 103 to 101" or "The Celtics blew past the Lakers 110–98 in overtime".

- Hockey: "The Kings skated past the Avalanche 5 to 4" or "The Wild posted a 3–2 sudden death (or overtime) win over the Rangers".

- Football: "The Rams knocked off the Jets 21 to 14" or "The Patriots played to a 24–24 tie with Green Bay".

- Soccer: "The L-A Galaxy beat the Seattle Sounders 5–2."

- Tennis: "Rafael Nadal beat Roger Federer 6–4, 3–6, 6–4 to win the XXX Tournament".

- Golf: "Tiger Woods won the XXX tournament coming in 3 under par".

Keep it just that simple. You don't need to go into any more detail than that unless you really know the sport.

You may also be asked to report on games that are going on at the very time that you are putting together your sports script. Again, keeping it simple will be the key to doing this successfully.

The wire service keeps a running 'Scoreboard' on games in progress. It will look something like this:

Just select the games you are interested in and write one quick line for each. Here are some examples:

- Baseball: "The Angels are leading the Yankees 3–2 in the third inning".

- Basketball: "The Lakers are trailing the Knicks 57–55 in the second period".

- Hockey: "The Ducks have skated out to a 6–3 lead over the Blackhawks after two periods".

- Football: "Dallas has jumped out to a first quarter 14 to nothing lead over Seattle".

- Soccer: "The New York Red Bulls are leading the Portland Timbers 3–2 in the 57th minute."

Note that in the football example, we substituted the portion of the team's locater for their nickname. You can do it either way or mix them up just to add some variation to your cast.

113

Time to Write

If you are adding games that are in progress into your script, you want to finish it as close to airtime as possible so that your scores are accurate.

If there are not a lot of games in progress when you are crafting your sports report, you will also find a variety of sports stories on the wires. This will include things like trades, streaks, team special events or even sometimes personal stories on the players. You can use any that look interesting in your sportscast and especially keep an eye out for information on your local teams.

You can also list games that will be coming up later in the day for your local teams. You will find the start times are listed in Eastern Standard Time, so be sure to change them to your local time when you write them into your cast.

Business

Unless you are into the stock market, this may be the most confusing of the group. The easiest way to do business reports if you are not comfortable with Wall Street is with a simple template that you will simply fill in with information from the wire service.

Here is what you might see on the wire service and how you can plug this info into your template while Wall Street is in session: "On Wall Street, the Dow is trading (up or down) _____ points, the NASDAQ (NAHZ-DAK) is (up or down) _____ points and the S-and-P-500 is (up or down) _____ points."

Trading concludes each weekday at 1pm Eastern Standard Time. After that, this is what you will see on the wires and how you can do an appropriate report: "On Wall Street today, the Dow closed (higher or lower) at a trading volume of _____, NASDAQ (NAHZ-DAK) ended the day (up or down) and the S-and-P-500 (gained or fell) by _____."

Again, simplicity is the key. Don't get fancy unless you understand what you are writing.

Traffic

The biggest problem with writing a traffic report is that the information can change very quickly and you are in the studio, not out on the road where

114

Other Types of News

you can see what is going on . . . but your audience is, so they will know if you are right or wrong. All you can do is be as accurate as possible.

How you will get information on the roads for a traffic report will vary greatly from city to city. In some cities, it is possible to go online and see the computer logs for whatever law enforcement agency covers the highways and freeways in real time. There is also a website, www.SigAlert. com, that is available in most metro areas. And of course there are a lot of other sites that cover traffic that you can access on the Internet or even on your phone.

The accuracy of these sites can be questionable. They are often based on information called in to them by listeners. Because people really depend on traffic reports and get really unhappy when they are incorrect, I prefer to use the law enforcement sites and then www.SigAlert.com to check for backed up traffic and other information.

Again, the key to a traffic report is simplicity. If you don't know the roads well or are reporting traffic for the first time, all you need to include in your cast is:

- The name of the highway, roadway or freeway. This can be the actual number that is used in your area or the name if that is more common.
- The location, such as what street or exchange the incident is closest to.
- The type of incident: an accident, stalled car, flooded road, road closure, etc.
- What lanes are blocked, if you know this.
- How far the traffic is backed up as a result. Again, only if you know this; if not just leave it out.

With that information, you can put together a simple but informative traffic report.

Here is an example (using Southern California freeways):

> There's an accident blocking the center lanes of the northbound Santa Ana freeway at Paramount. It's backing traffic up to Beach Boulevard. A stalled car is in the left lane of the southbound Long Beach freeway at Atlantic. The eastbound 91 is slow starting at Norwalk because of a crash that is on the righthand shoulder ahead at Harbor. And there is

Time to Write

> roadwork on the connector from the eastbound 134 to the southbound 405 that has it down to just one lane.

Simple, clear and concise. That's what your audience needs when they are deciding what route to take as they try to get somewhere without getting tied up in traffic.

Note that the order that various components of each item changed from line to line. This is so the report would not sound like a 'laundry list' when read.

Read the following example out loud and you will see that without changing the elements you will very quickly settle into a very unattractive rhythm:

> There's an accident on the northbound Santa Ana Freeway at Paramount blocking the center lanes and backing traffic up to Beach Boulevard. There's a stalled car on the southbound Long Beach Freeway at Atlantic in the left lane. There's a crash on the eastbound 91 at Harbor on the right shoulder slowing traffic from Norwalk.

While this has all the pertinent information and is an acceptable traffic report, the rhythm that the writing forces is not pleasant to hear. Just move the pieces around a bit and the rhythm disappears.

Weather

No matter what part of the country you are in, weather is a big deal. Knowing what to expect helps people figure out what kind of clothes to wear and how early they should leave for work.

Meteorologists know all kinds of interesting information about why certain types of weather patterns are happening, but again, this is specialized information that not many of us have. So we will again apply a very simple formula to doing the weather.

The wire services will have a great many charts and a lot of information in their weather cue and it can be very confusing. I prefer one of several weather forecasting websites because the information is much easier to understand and use quickly. My favorite is www.wunderground.com.

116

Other Types of News

All we are basically looking for is the following:

- The sky condition: sunny, cloudy, mostly cloudy, foggy, etc.
- The conditions: raining, windy, snowing, etc.
- The expected temperature for the day.
- The current temperatures for several cities in the station's coverage area and ending with the city that the station itself is in.

Here is an example of a simple weathercast:

> Expect a windy and rainy day today. Mostly cloudy with a 60-percent chance of rain. Highs today should be in the upper 50s to the upper 60s. Right now, it's 47 in Long Beach, 52 in North Hollywood and 53 degrees here in Los Angeles.

You really don't need much more than this for a weathercast to add to the end of your newscast. Of course, weather can change very rapidly, so you will want to check and update your weathercast accordingly before you use it in subsequent newscasts throughout the day.

Points to Remember

- The key to doing sports, business, traffic and weather is to keep it simple.
- Beyond the basics, don't add more to your casts than you actually understand yourself.
- The time listed on wire stories will always be in Eastern Standard Time. You will need to change these to your local time before using them on the air to avoid confusing your audience.

Exercises

1. Write a 30-second Sports report using the following information. Consider that these scores are finals:
   - Dodgers 4 Brewers 2
   - Yankees 5 Angels 1

Time to Write

- Lakers 111 Jazz 107
- Celtics 98 Warriors 85
- Kings 8 Blues 5
- Ducks 3 Sharks 2

2. Write a 30-second Business report using the following information:
   - The Dow closed up 38 points at 18,653
   - The NASDAQ gained 52
   - The S-and-P 500 fell 48

3. Write a 30-second Traffic report using the following information:
   - Accident on the northbound 5 Freeway at Main on the right shoulder
   - Stalled car in the fast lane of southbound 138 at Grand
   - Accident blocking three lanes of the eastbound Highway 91 Freeway at Cook Avenue
   - Stalled truck blocking the Atlantic offramp from the northbound 210 Freeway

4. Write a 30-second Weather report using the following information:
   - Sunny today
   - Temperatures in the low 80s at the beaches
   - Temperatures inland in the low 90s
   - Breezes in the afternoon
   - Clear overnight
   - Lows in the 50s

> *I always told new people about getting traffic info and doing the report, "You have to do it good enough, fast enough".*
> —Alexander Piela – Former Director of Operations,
> Metro Traffic Control, Lewes, Delaware

PART

IV

Working with Audio and Video

FUN FUN PHOTO/shutterstock.com

14 | Types of Audio and Video

In this Chapter

- Proper Use of Audio and Video
- Wire-generated Audio and Video
- Station-gathered Audio and Video
- Ambient Sound and B-Roll

Increase Your Industry Vocabulary

- Audio cuts (also called sound bites, sound, cuts, actualities) – These are short bits of interviews that can be included in stories that are written by the station writers
- B-Roll – This video is unedited sound from the scene of news. It is video that can be used to set the atmosphere for a story
- Q & A session – Q & A stands for Question and Answer. This audio will be of a question and answer session between an AP reporter or stringer and someone he or she is interviewing about a particular story. You will clearly hear both of them in the audio
- Raw sound (also called ambient, natural or nat sound) – This audio is unedited sound from the scene of news. It is most often used as background sound
- Scener – This is a piece that sets the scene of a news event that will be happening later

121

Working with Audio and Video

- Voicers – This is a piece that uses only the reporter. There are no actualities
- Wraps – These are created and voiced by AP reporters or freelance stringers and come with an anchor lead.

 ## Proper Use of Audio and Video

There is a phrase in radio broadcasting. It's "sound for the sake of sound". It means don't add sound to a story just so there is some sound in it. The sound you add has to have a purpose in order to be included in the story. The same can be said for video. If the audio or video doesn't add to the telling of the story, then it should be left out.

That is the true purpose of audio or video in news stories... to enhance the story, to make the audience feel like they are there at the scene of news and to help them to understand the story. If your audio or video does not do that, it's unnecessary.

There are a number of places where we can get these resources. There are companies that provide audio and video to media outlets or stations can get them on their own. Today, some organizations are also pulling sound and video from social media. This can be very risky to do though. The sound of video could be faked or there may be copyright issues. Bottom line, it's not a good idea.

 ## Wire-generated Audio and Video

Just as it is with written content, several of the wire services also provide audio and video for use by radio and television stations. AP or the Associated Press is a major source of video and audio for radio and television news outlets. It is a service that is in addition to the wire copy and stations have to subscribe in order to gain access to it. With that subscription, they are free to use those resources in any way they wish without having to give credit to AP. Their subscription gives them the right to use this otherwise copyrighted material. In the cases of wraps, voicers, sceners and Q & A sessions, they feature an AP reporter or freelance stringer. These pros can be used on any subscribing station's air without any permission or

Types of Audio and Video

payment needed. The pieces are ready to air with no editing or additional production work required.

The audio and video coordinate with the stories AP is covering. Again, just like with the wire stories, new audio and video is constantly being filed 24/7.

These resources come in a variety of forms. For radio these include:

- Audio cuts (also called sound bites, sound, cuts, actualities) – These can be included in stories that are written by the station writers.

- Wraps – These are created and voiced by AP reporters or freelance stringers and come with an anchor lead. They are ready to simply drop into a newscast.

- Voicers – These work exactly as a wrap does. The only difference is that within the pre-recorded report there is no actuality. It is entirely the voice of the reporter. Voicers also come with a pre-written anchor lead.

- Scener – This is generally a voicer although it can also be a wrap. It could be considered a pre-story. It is done in advance of an event that is expected shortly such as a court verdict. It's a way of keeping a story in the news before there really is any news to actually report yet.

- Q & A session – Q & A stands for Question and Answer. This audio will be of a question and answer session between an AP reporter or stringer and someone he or she is interviewing about a particular story. You will clearly hear both of them in the audio. The Q & A session comes with a pre-written lead that can be used in the story to introduce the audio. The story itself will be written by someone at the station.

- Raw sound (also called ambient, natural or nat sound) – This audio is unedited sound from the scene of news. It is background sound that can be used to set the atmosphere for a story or may be used under the actual voicing of the story by either the reporter or the anchor. It is often quite long and can be edited to any length necessary. If the story were about a fire, this might be audio of the fire trucks and their sirens, the flames, the water being used to put out the fire, etc.

For TV, the forms are pretty much the same. They include:

- Wraps – This is a self-contained video piece featuring an AP reporter or freelance stringer and comes with an anchor lead. They will contain a

123

Working with Audio and Video

video cut from an interview and video from the scene of the story. They are ready to simply drop into a newscast.

- Voicers – These work exactly as a wrap does. They are self-contained. The only difference is that they will not contain an additional interview video cut. They will feature only the reporter or stringer. Voicers also come with a pre-written anchor lead.

- Scener – This is generally a voicer although it can also be a wrap. It could be considered a pre-story. It is done in advance of an event that is expected shortly such as a court verdict. It's a way of keeping a story in the news before there really is any news to actually report yet. It will feature video from the scene of the upcoming event.

- Q & A session – Q & A stands for Question and Answer. This video will be of an AP reporter or stringer interviewing someone involved in the story that they are covering. You will clearly hear and see both of them. The Q & A session comes with a pre-written lead that can be used in the story to introduce the audio. The story itself will be written by someone at the station.

- B-Roll – This video is unedited sound from the scene of news. It is video that can be used to set the atmosphere for a story. It generally does not have sound so that it can be used under the actual voicing of the story by either the reporter or the anchor. It is generally used at the beginning of the piece or between the various interviews as a background.

Station-gathered Audio and Video

Not all the stories that we want to cover are also being covered by AP, so we will be collecting a lot of sound ourselves.

This audio and video is most often acquired by going to the scene of the story and shooting or recording it. It can then be used by a reporter in a live shot, added to a piece that is going to be recorded for later use or sent back into the station electronically so that it can be used in creating a story in-house.

In radio, we can also get sound through interviews done over the phone. These interviews can be done live on the air with an anchor or reporter or the reporter can pre-record the interview over the phone with the newsmaker and then edit it to be used in pieces written by in-house writers.

Ambient Sound and B-Roll

We want our audience to experience the stories we report on along with us. Using ambient sound in radio and B-Roll for TV are among the strongest ways that we can do this.

In radio, it allows the listener to 'hear' what people are experiencing on the scene. Imagine the difference in impact a story about a parade would have if you could hear the marching bands and the people cheering versus a story where the reporter just told you about it.

When we use sound to help tell the story, we are using a radio trick called 'theater of the mind' that was developed back in the early days of radio when radio dramas were all the rage. The sound helped the listener to 'see' the story. Although we rarely perform radio dramas anymore, this technique is still very useful in creating powerful stories for radio news.

B-Roll in television news is also used to set the feeling of the story and to give viewers an additional look at what is going on. During breaking news, it is easy to decide what to shoot, but in a more static story, a good visual imagination is necessary. Let's say you were doing a story about a flood. While you could tell your listeners how bad the situation was, how high the water was, how cars were being washed away . . . it would have a lot more impact if they could see it for themselves. This is the advantage that B-Roll provides.

In both cases, radio and television, the addition of ambient sound and B-Roll brings stories to life. They also add additional voices and sound to our newscasts. They are opportunities to enhance our storytelling abilities and should be used whenever possible.

Points to Remember

- Audio and video should be used only when it actually will enhance the telling of the story.

Working with Audio and Video

- Several wire services supply audio and video to subscribing stations.
- Audio and video should be used wherever possible to help the audience understand the story.

Exercises

1. What kind of ambient sound would you want to get for the following stories? Make a list of at least two for each story:
   - A fire
   - A record release party
   - A rain storm
   - A baseball game
   - The grand opening of a park
   - A protest
   - Construction on a new building
   - A marathon
   - The wedding of a famous couple
   - A casino robbery

2. What kind of B-Roll would you want to get for the following stories? Make a list of at least two for each story:
   - An elementary school that will soon be closing
   - A brush fire
   - A classic car show
   - The end of a police chase
   - The grand opening of new shopping center
   - A college graduation
   - A whale watching experience
   - A story about circuses being banned
   - The opening of a new train station
   - A movie premiere

In radio, start your story with short interesting facts, then add color to it by painting a word picture of what you see and the expressed emotions of those involved. Wrap it up with a creative retelling of the core information.

—John Brooks – Former Reporter with KNX, KFWB, KVEN, KHAY and WARC

15 | Effective Interviewing

In this Chapter

- Preparing for the Interview
- Make It Interesting
- Asking the Right Questions
- Asking the Hard Questions
- Getting Too Much Information

Increase Your Industry Vocabulary

- Bullet points – A list of short ideas or things that you want to make sure to ask during an interview
- Command center – A location at the scene of news which is a centralized location for first responders
- First responders – Law enforcement, fire, paramedics, etc. Emergency personnel who are often the first ones on the scene of a crime or natural disaster
- Follow-up – The question you ask based on the answer given to a previous question
- Public Information Officer (PIO) – The person who is charged with working with the media. Most law enforcement, fire and military organizations have PIOs.

128

Effective Interviewing

Interviews are key to news. It is much more interesting to hear someone actually involved in the story tell us about it than it is to hear an anchor or reporter reading from a script. But interviews are not nearly as easy as they appear to be.

There is a misconception about the 'rules' to be followed during an interview. Most people think it is a simple Q & A; the reporter or anchor asks the question and the person being interviewed answers it.

While that's not actually wrong, it certainly is not the best way to do an interview. It sounds more like an interrogation. It yields nothing more than what the reporter is going for. And since he or she is not the expert on the topic or the situation, some very important and interesting information can easily be missed.

A better way to look at an interview is as a conversation. After all, that's what it really is. You actually do interviews, of sort, every day of your life. When you ask a friend what they did over the weekend, you are doing an interview. You will listen to their answer and ask follow-up questions to find out what you want to know until you are satisfied that you know enough to stop asking.

That's a conversation and there is no reason that we cannot do our professional interviews in much the same way. It's an exchange of information and there is nothing wrong with you giving some information as well, perhaps during the course of the interview relating information about a similar event or saying how something would make you feel. You can get a little personal without losing your professional edge.

If you can change the tone of the interview from something formal to simply a conversation you will get much better answers and that will make for a much better story.

It's a technique I have been employing for years and I have actually had people tell me at the end of the interview, "that was the most satisfying interview I have ever been involved in. I actually got to tell you what I wanted you to know about my story." Not only is that a great compliment, but I also got some great audio out of the interview as a result.

Preparing for the Interview

Preparing for an interview for a news story is different from preparing for an enterprise story interview such as we did in Chapter 10. In that preparation,

129

Working with Audio and Video

we had little actual material ahead of time to use. In addition, because we chose the story, we may go into it knowing quite a bit more about the topic than we would a regular news story.

For regular news interviews, we start with getting details on the story. We may also need to determine who to interview. With some stories this is obvious; in others it may take some understanding of the story to figure out who would have the most important information and give us the best perspective.

Sometimes you can't interview the person at the scene even though they would be your obvious first choice. With organizations like law enforcement, military and fire, the officer or firefighter on the scene is not authorized to talk to the media. Depending on the situation, they may be able to give you some details 'off the record' but they will not go on mic or on camera. In these cases, you will be directed to a PIO (Public Information Officer) for the actual interview. If there is a command center at the scene, this would be the first place to try and contact them. If there is not a command center, you will likely find them at the organization's office or headquarters.

It's important to remember that PIOs are working with all media. You may have to wait a while for them to get to you to make a comment. Be patient; while they know it is important for you to get your interview so you can take your story to air, they have a lot to deal with. Most of the people in this position do a great job of servicing the media as quickly as they possibly can.

We also need to understand the story enough to know what to ask. While our interview is going to mirror a conversation, you are still going to be the one leading it. Remember, we work fast in the news business and you probably won't have a lot of time to do much research. You will likely just have time to check out the wire copy or the press release. This may make you feel very awkward or unprepared at first, but the more often you do it, the more you will learn to think on your feet.

It is also very helpful to know ahead of the interview what you are going to end up doing with it. Of course, you are going to use it on the air, but in what form? How many pieces and what type? Depending on the station that you work for, you probably will be doing several sides of the story. Remember, sides means versions. Your station may want a wrap and two voice cut stories. That means you will need three good cuts from the interview.

Effective Interviewing

Make It Interesting

News is made up of big stories and not so big stories. Some stories are very interesting and some, well, not so much. No matter which type of story you are assigned, it is up to you to make it interesting to your listeners and viewers.

You can do this through the angle you take to the story. Let's take the extremely mundane story about an area getting a new area code. You probably would groan if you saw that come up in your assignments for the day. While it's important, it's boring. Or is it?

Most reporters will take pretty much the same approach to this story and simply talk to someone from the group behind the area code change. In California, that would be the Public Utilities Commission. They would probably ask:

- What is the new area code?

- What area does it cover?

- Why is that area getting a new area code?

- When does it go into effect?

Informative, but boring. And especially boring if you don't live in the area getting that new area code. But what if you take a much different approach to the story? You do need to ask the previous questions, but let's make the angle of the story the effect the new area code will have. Perhaps talk to a shop owner in the area and ask:

- What will you have to do when the new area code takes effect? (They will probably have to get new invoices, change their business cards, maybe even buy a new sign for outside their business if their current one has their phone number on it.)

- What will all that cost?

You might also talk to someone who lives in a neighborhood where the area code is changing. You can probably find someone at the local grocery store to talk to. You might ask them:

131

- What do you think of the upcoming area code change? (They might not even know about it yet.)
- How hard will it be to remember another area code?
- How will you let your friends outside the area know that they have to dial a new area code to reach you?

It's still not the most exciting story ever, but with a little creative thought, it is more interesting than it started out to be. And your story on this new area code will certainly sound different from every other station in town that probably also covered it today.

Asking the Right Questions

The first question I always ask a person is their name. It may sound silly, but it is imperative that you get this right. So I will always ask them to say their name into the mic. This way I am sure I get the pronunciation right. I will also ask them to spell it even if it is a common name. Even common names can have unconventional spellings. And finally, I ask them to state their title, if they have one. You need to have this information and it needs to be accurate. You may be using it in a graphic on TV or in the caption for a piece on social media. People are very protective over their names, as well they should be, and it is very insulting for a person's name to be incorrectly spelled or said. The same can be said for a title. Titles mean a lot to some people so they should mean a lot to you too.

During the interview, the responses you get are only going to be as good as the questions that you ask. If you ask a question that can be answered with a yes or a no, that is exactly what you will probably get and that makes for very poor audio or video. Ask questions that force the person being interviewed to actually give you information.

At the same time, avoid giving the answer to the question in the question itself. This can happen if you know too much about the story. Keep your questions brief and to the point and leave room for the person you are talking with to answer.

Your job as an interviewer is to get good audio or video for your story. Good means informative and interesting. As we know, not every story is interesting and not every person you interview is going to be a good interviewee.

Effective Interviewing

It's up to you to determine the right questions to ask. The right questions are what your listener or viewer would want to know about this story if they were asking the questions. But they aren't, so it's up to you to ask them.

There is a saying that there are no dumb questions. While that's not entirely true, we've all probably heard some pretty stupid ones. But when it comes to doing an interview, if you do not understand something that is said in an answer, you should ask what it means. Chances are that if you don't know what something means, your audience will not know either. If you don't ask, it's going to be hard to properly use that portion of the interview in your story and if you do, it could be very confusing to your audience.

Many reporters rely on the Five W's and an H . . . who, what, when, where, why and how. But you probably already know the majority of those facts from your research prior to the interview.

The interview is the opportunity to get information outside of those basics. Take it from the position of, "If I were just now hearing about this, what would I want to know?"

If it's a brush fire, you would already know who is on the scene, how many acres it is, how many homes are being threatened, when it started, where it's located. You probably wouldn't know yet how it started. So what can you ask? What would your audience ask?

- Evacuations – what area is evacuated and where are people going?
- Large animals – animals like horses can rarely be taken to evacuation centers for humans; where are these types of animals being housed?
- Firefighting effort – how is the fire being fought? From the ground? The air? How many gallons do those water dropping planes carry?
- Weather conditions – are they helping or hindering the firefighters?
- The fire zone – what types of structures are being threatened? Is there something other than homes or businesses in the area (like landmarks, transmission lines, etc.)? What type of terrain is it?
- History – when did this area last burn?

You now have a lot more to go with for your story than most of the other reporters on the scene. This is also going to be beneficial to you if you have to file multiple sides of the story or you need to do this story over the

Working with Audio and Video

course of several news cycles. Each version or every time you do the story, it will now be a little bit different and be fresh to your audience.

Asking the Hard Questions

Nobody likes to ask or answer the hard questions, but to do the news properly sometimes they have to be asked.

We looked at the hardest questions of all to ask . . . questions to victims or the families of victims . . . in Chapter 4 on Ethical and Moral Newswriting. But by the very nature of news, there will be plenty of other situations where you will need to ask equally difficult questions.

There is no easy way to learn to ask them. You simply need to use compassion and courtesy when asking and be prepared for a response that sometimes is not what you hoped it will be.

Getting Too Much Information

Generally we do not have a lot of time to get these interviews and in a way that is a good thing. You don't want to have hours of audio or video to sort through when you start to prepare your story.

You need to keep the interview going until you have enough information to write and produce the story. Even if you have a good amount of detail going into the interview, new and more up-to-date information is likely to come out during the course of talking with the person you are interviewing. You can take that information and use it in your writing.

Earlier in this chapter, we talked about the need to know going into the interview what you are going to do with it. If you know ahead of time how many pieces you are going to create and what kind, you will know how much of the interview you are actually going to use. This can save you a lot of time and effort.

For example, if you know that you are going to have a need for three cuts of the interview, you need to be listening during the interview for three good cuts. You can take a quick look at your recording device or camera and make a note of the position on the counter so you can go back and find them quickly and easily. Once you have those cuts, you don't necessarily

134

Effective Interviewing

want to immediately end the interview. It's always a good idea to get a few more just so you have additional material to work with.

Probably the most important question I ever learned to ask is "Is there anything else that you would like to tell me?" Even with the most conversational interview, people will tend to only answer what they are asked. Often, there is something that they really want to tell you about, but you didn't ask, so it goes unsaid. Some of the best audio and video that I have ever gotten has come from asking that question. Sometimes they say that everything they wanted to get out was covered and you can end the interview, but other times you get something fantastic that no other reporter will get.

Interviewing is a skill unto itself and it takes time to develop, just like any other skill. Keep your mind open and be curious and you will find something interesting in just about any interview that you do.

Points to Remember

- Most first responders are not allowed to talk to the media. You will likely need to talk to the PIO.

- Most situations that warrant a response by first responders will have a command center which will be your first stop when looking for information and interviews.

- You are not their first priority so you may have to wait for your interview.

- It's a good idea to know how many pieces you are expected to create with your interview so you know how much audio or video you will need.

- If you don't understand something in the interview, chances are your audience won't either. Ask the person you are interviewing to explain it for you.

Exercises

1. Select a famous person that you would like to interview. Create a bullet point list that you would use in the interview. Your list should include at least ten bullet points.

135

Working with Audio and Video

2. Write a follow-up question to the following interview quotes:

- "I have been working for the company for the last 20 years, but I have also written two books."

- "The new road will take much longer than anticipated to open. We're thinking about two to three more weeks."

- "Our new policy will make getting the help to the people who need it much quicker. It's something that we've been trying to make happen for years."

- "We think that we have arrested everyone involved based on what we have learned so far. We also recovered at least 200-thousand-dollars in what appears to be stolen merchandise."

- "The accident on the freeway will require us to bring in a big rig tow. Until we can do that, at least three lanes will be blocked and there is a big back-up already."

- "The bird has been on the endangered species list for some time and we don't see its situation improving any time soon. There are just too many issues that are keeping the species from thriving."

- "If you are going camping this summer, we are urging people to make sure they understand the rules in the national parks. The rules aren't there just because we wanted to make some rules. They are crucial to the ability for us to maintain the parks and keep them open for people to use."

- "The new sales tax goes into effect next month. It will raise an estimated 2-million a year to help the city's homeless population."

- "Even though only one small shark was spotted, we've closed the beaches until we are sure that the water is safe for people to go in it."

- "Under the new law, teen-age drivers will not be able to use their cellphones behind the wheel at all during the first six months that they have a license."

136

Even if you want to become an engineer or an operations person and not a broadcast radio or TV reporter you are part of a team effort. Making sure your reporters can get stories from the field back to the studio in real time, making sure your station stays on the air so the news can get to the public, and making sure your station is ready during major power and Internet outages so it can stay on the air all support the team effort to get the news out. You can help make a positive impact on people's lives, and occasionally deliver life saving information to a public at risk. The reward: The pride of being a valuable and productive team member.

—Richard Rudman – Director of Engineering,
KFWB, Los Angeles – 1975–2002

Don't speculate. Invest some time in learning about first responders.

—Rod Bernsen – Fox News, Fox 11 News,
CNN Headline News, KFI, WMTR-AM
and retired LAPD Sergeant

16 | Selecting and Writing with Interview Clips

In this Chapter

- Finding the Right Cut
- Writing In and Out of Cuts for Radio
- Working In and Around Cuts for Television
- Working with Multiple Cuts
- Getting Information from the Interview
- Using Ambient Sound

Increase Your Industry Vocabulary

- A-Roll – Video cuts from an interview
- Ambient sound – The sounds from the scene of news. Also called natural (nat) sound
- Anchor tag – A few sentences to be read by the anchor following a pre-recorded piece. It usually contains information that deals with numbers or times and is not included in the recorded story because it could make it unusable if the information changes
- Incue – The first few words of a voice cut
- Lead in – A sentence that either introduces a cut in an actuality story or a wrap. It identifies the speaker in the actuality and provides a smooth transition from the person reading the story into the piece

138

Selecting and Writing with Interview Clips

- Lock out – A standard phrase used by reporters to close out any live or recorded piece. It includes their name as well as the name of the station. It might also include the station's slogan

- Outcue – The last few words of a voice cut. It's put in the story as a cue to let the person reading the story know what they are listening for

- SFX – Sound effects (also know as EFX)

- TRT – Total Run Time: The length of an audio or video cut

- VO (Voice Over) – The copy that will be read by a TV reporter or anchor

You've done your interview and learned all you can about your story, or you've pulled available sound or video from AP. Now it's time to incorporate it into your writing.

Here is where the art comes in and perhaps some frustration along with it. There are no rules for how you use sound or video in your story. I used the word 'art' because it truly is. You are creating with sound or video and your final story will not be the same as anyone else's who might be doing the same story.

It doesn't take much longer to be creative than it does to be average. You can do exactly what is required or you can do something special; not every time, but it's fun to do the unexpected every now and again.

Finding the Right Cut

What came first, the chicken or the egg? It's an age-old question that we may never get the answer to. So it is with working with video or audio in a news setting.

Some people prefer to start to write their story and then add the audio or video clip to it, making whatever adjustments are necessary. This can work. Others, myself included, prefer to pull the audio or video cuts first and then write the story around them. Of course, if you are working with AP or otherwise pre-generated sound, you will already have your cuts.

Either way is fine; there is no right way or wrong way. All that matters is that you find which way helps you make an amazing final piece.

The cuts you select should say something important in connection with your story. Let your audio or video selection tell the story itself; you just fill in around it with the details. Your interview cuts should have the spotlight.

139

Working with Audio and Video

 # Writing In and Out of Cuts for Radio

You want your interview pieces to flow with the story, not seem like something just stuck in the middle of it. To make this happen, you need to correctly write into and out of the cuts.

How we do this has gradually been changing over the past few years but we are going to look at best practices in how we work with our cuts.

When using AP audio or video, the lead-in is already provided for you. The lead-in is the line that immediately precedes the interview cut. You don't have to use it at all or you can re-write it. The choice is up to you.

When you are working with audio or video that you have collected yourself, the lead-in becomes your responsibility. One mistake that beginners often make is that they say exactly what is in the cut in the lead-in.

An example of this would be:

> Lead-in: Mayor John Smith said the downtown area will benefit greatly from the new rail service.
>
> Cut audio: The new rail service will benefit the entire downtown area.

That would sound terrible on the air. It sounds like the reporter has no idea what is in the cut. It's an easy fix though, even with very little additional information:

> Lead-in: Mayor John Smith says he expects good things to come from the new rail line.
>
> Cut audio: The new rail service will benefit the entire downtown area.

If you're stuck on the lead-in, a clever way to figure it out is to listen to what was said on the interview just before the cut that you chose to use in your story. That will often give you something that will dovetail perfectly into your cut.

It is very easy to turn a reader into an actuality story once the actuality becomes available. Starting with a reader allows the story to get on the air quickly and then to be updated later.

Let's take a reader script from Chapter 7 and turn it into an actuality story. You will also see how to express the actuality in the script.

Here is the reader version:

> Firefighters were on the scene of a blaze at John's Sandwich Shop in Long Beach last night within ten minutes of it being reported, but still weren't in time to stop the fire from destroying the shop. The store's employees are being credited with thinking fast and getting customers out quickly after smoke started billowing out of an oven that was used to bake bread in the back of the store. The restaurant suffered at least 30-thousand-dollars in damage. It's not clear if the popular neighborhood hang-out will be rebuilt. Investigators are working to determine what exactly caused the fire.

Now let's add this actuality. It's from one of the store's employees, Jeff Cassidy, and is 10-seconds long: "I knew there wasn't much time. The smoke was really starting to get thick. These customers are our friends. They're like family to most of us. We just wanted to make sure everyone was safe."

This is how the script looks as an actuality story for radio:

> Firefighters were on the scene of a blaze at John's Sandwich Shop in Long Beach last night within ten minutes of it being reported, but still weren't in time to stop the fire from destroying the shop. The store's employees are being credited with thinking fast and getting customers out quickly. Jeff Cassidy has worked at John's for five years.
>
> outcue: everyone was safe.
> TRT: 10
>
> The smoke was coming from an oven that was used to bake bread in the back of the store. The restaurant suffered at least 30-thousand-dollars in damage. It's not clear if the popular neighborhood hang-out will be rebuilt. Investigators are working to determine what exactly caused the fire.

We added a lead-in that introduces who is speaking in the actuality as well as a quick line to tie the cut into the story. We also noted the final three words of the actuality. This is so whoever is reading the story knows

Working with Audio and Video

what to listen for as a cue to start reading the copy again. And we put in the length of the cut, Total Run Time (TRT), so that it can be counted into the total length of the story.

Just a note on lead-ins for your actualities: You may hear the identification of the speaker sometimes put in after the cut. This is not the best practice. It makes much more sense to your audience to know who they are hearing and what their connection is to the story before the actuality is heard or seen.

Here is how our actuality script would look if it was turned into a wrap for radio:

(This would be read by the anchor)

Firefighters were on the scene of a blaze at John's Sandwich Shop in Long Beach last night within ten minutes of it being reported, but KXYZ's Tammy Trujillo says they weren't in time.

(This is the wrap)

By the time crews arrived, John's was pretty much destroyed. The store's employees are being credited with thinking fast and getting customers out quickly. Jeff Cassidy has worked at John's for five years.

> outcue: everyone was safe.
> TRT: 10

The smoke was coming from an oven that was used to bake bread in the back of the store. The restaurant suffered at least 30-thousand-dollars in damage. It's not clear if the popular neighborhood hang-out will be rebuilt. Investigators are working to determine what exactly caused the fire. Tammy Trujillo, KXYZ News for the Southland.

Just like the outcue on the cut is a cue for whoever is reading the story to start reading the rest of the copy, the lock out is a cue for whoever is anchoring to move on to the next story. Lock outs are specific to each station and are generally created by the News or Program Director.

142

Selecting and Writing with Interview Clips

The wrap is generally not done live on the air although it can be. Most often it is recorded.

Working In and Around Cuts for Television

Using pieces of your video interview is not that much different from using your audio cuts. You want to work them around the copy that you or the reporter will read.

Let's take our radio story and just for fun, we'll give it a couple of extra interview cuts and even some B-Roll.

How you set up your script is different (see Table 16.1).

Table 16.1 Sample TV News Script

Timing	Video	Audio
0:00–0:10	**B-Roll:** Shot of the burned out sandwich shop	**VO:** Firefighters were on the scene of a blaze at John's Sandwich Shop in Long Beach last night within ten minutes of it being reported, but still weren't in time to stop the fire from destroying the shop.
0:10–0:16	**B-Roll:** Shot of employees and customers outside of the shop	**VO:** The store's employees are being credited with thinking fast and getting customers out quickly.
0:16–0:26	**A-Roll:** Interview cut with Jeff Cassidy	**Jeff Cassidy:** I knew there wasn't much time. The smoke was really starting to get thick. These customers are our friends. They're like family to most of us. We just wanted to make sure everyone was safe.
0:26–0:32	**B-Roll:** Shot of fire trucks on the street outside the restaurant	**VO:** Several employees say the smoke was coming from an oven that was used to bake bread in the back of the store.
0:36–0:44	**A-Roll:** Interview with Fire Captain Bruce Johnson	**Fire Captain Bruce Johnson:** The restaurant suffered at least 30-thousand-dollars in damage. The fire was so hot that by the time we got here there was very little we could do to save any part of it.
0:44–0:52	**B-Roll:** Shot of the partially burned store sign	**VO:** It's not clear if the popular neighborhood hang-out will be rebuilt. Investigators are working to determine what exactly caused the fire.

Working with Audio and Video

You may have noticed that unlike in the radio script, we didn't verbally introduce the speakers in the two interview cuts. In television, their identities will appear on the screen as they are shown, so there is no need to write them into the script.

Working with Multiple Cuts

If you have several actualities, you would simply add the next one in the story wherever it fits and make the same notation as we did in this example. If the actuality is with the same person as the first one, you don't need to re-identify the speaker but you will need to use at least one line of copy between the two cuts. If it is with a different person, you will need to write a lead-in that introduces this new person and flows into the cut.

Getting Information from the Interview

Sometimes, no matter how much we research a story, we come up short on details when we sit down to write and put it together. One neat little trick I learned a while ago is to listen to the entire interview. You already know that you are only going to be using a small portion of it for your actualities. But the rest of it is full of information that you can use to build your story. It also may have some good details that you can include that were not in the wire copy, press release or other source material that you used for the story.

Using Ambient Sound

Several times we have talked about using ambient or nat sound in our stories. If there is sound associated with your story, you should use it, especially in radio. There are no rules about how you use it. The sound can be at the beginning of the piece and open it, run underneath the entire length of the piece or just under a portion of it.

When you use ambient sound, be very careful about the levels. You want to make sure your audience can hear it, but you don't want it to drown out the voice or interview track or make it hard to understand.

Selecting and Writing with Interview Clips

One story I was assigned as a reporter started out as a real 'who cares', or at least that is how it looked to me.

I was assigned to do a story on the winner of a contest held to find a modern day Scarlett O'Hara, the heroine of the classic film _Gone with the Wind_. I love classic movies, but frankly this one left me cold. I had audio of the winner with her response to the famous quote at the end of the movie uttered by her love interest Rhett Butler, "Frankly, my dear, I don't give a damn."

Fortunately, I only had to do one side of this story but I still was looking for something to give it a little more oomph! I finally came up with the idea of using the actual audio from the movie of Rhett Butler saying the line to open the piece followed by the winner's response. Because of Fair Use Law, I was able to use this copyright piece of the movie with no problem. We looked at Fair Use in Chapter 3 of this book.

This could have also been done with a video clip of the movie then moving to a shot of the winner saying her line.

The rest of the story was a voicer by me with details about the contest itself. Starting with audio or video and using it to actually interact with the winner's cut was something rather unusual, but it sounded good and turned out really well.

Points to Remember

- The cuts you pull from your interview should have content that will add to the story.

- Your interview can give you additional information to use in the creation of your story.

- Use ambient or natural sound to enhance your story. You can use it in any way you want; there are no rules except to watch your levels.

- There are other kinds of sound you can add to your story, but you need to make sure you observe copyright laws if you use them.

- When using interview cuts in a radio story, you must identify the speaker in your script. In television stories, the identification will be on the screen.

Working with Audio and Video

Exercises

1. Add the following cuts to these readers to turn them into radio actuality stories. You may have to re-write the copy slightly in order to seamlessly use the actualities:

> a. Tax day is coming up fast... and the tax scammers are ramping up their efforts to get a piece of the action. City Police are warning about people getting calls from someone saying they're from the IRS, telling them they owe back taxes and threatening them if they don't pay up over the phone. The caller gives them specific instructions on how to wire the money to what appears to be an IRS bank account. If you get such a call, hang up. The IRS doesn't call people who owe taxes, it sends a letter.
>
> Cut: Sergeant Jim Thompson TRT: 10
>
> "We don't want people to be taken. There are a lot of unethical individuals right now who are preying on people. They're basically using fear tactics to get people to do what they want them to do."
>
> b. The circus may not be coming to town for much longer. The Board of Supervisors is considering a proposal that would ban the use of exotic animals in circuses in Caldwell County. There would be some exceptions such as for rodeos and accredited zoos. It's something lawmakers have been talking about for the past several years, but say the recent death of a circus tiger after a performance on the East Coast got them thinking about it again. Even if the ban is approved, the Wildman Circus will still perform locally as scheduled in late September.
>
> Cut: Supervisor David Jones TRT: 18
>
> "I think all of us on the board love animals and that is the main reason that we are looking at this ban. For years there has been growing evidence that animals used in circuses and other traveling shows are mistreated. We think that by

Selecting and Writing with Interview Clips

banning these shows as other counties have already done, it will result in more of these animals being sent to sanctuaries to live as they should."

2. Turn your two radio actuality stories into television stories. You may have to re-write the content slightly. You have the following selection of B-Roll to use:

Tax Story

- :07 Shot of the front of the police station
- :06 Shot of a calendar with April 15 circled on it
- :06 Shot of a mailbox
- :04 Shot of an IRS form

Circus Story

- :06 Shot of performing tigers
- :07 Shot of a circus tent
- :08 Shot of performing tigers
- :04 Shot of a billboard for the circus

First, if you want to go into an honorable profession that gives you the opportunity to help people who need it and expose those who take advantage of the public trust . . . in addition to providing you with a continuing education every day . . . you will never be disappointed. If you take a broadcast job just to get famous or be rich, you will never be happy.
> —John Beard – Morning Anchor, WGRZ-TV,
> Buffalo-Toronto

My guide has always been "it's never about you". When you convince yourself it is, don't report it. No one cares about your commentary unless that is your role.
> —Michael Means – KGU Talk Radio Honolulu –
> KIK FM / KOW FM / KSDO Vice President GM –
> KABC/KMPC (Radio Disney) Sales Manager – KLAA
> Angels Baseball Radio Sales Manager

PART

Social and Multi-media News

niroworld/shutterstock.com

Writing for Internet Usage

17

In this Chapter

- Style Differences
- Content Curation
- Spotting Fake News Sites
- Proper Attribution
- Links to Other Media
- Accuracy, Reliability and Responsibility

Increasing Your Industry Vocabulary

- Aggregators – Sites that do not originate material, but gather it from other sites
- Content curation – The process of gathering information relevant to a particular topic or area of interest

Social and multi-media are now a part of the news effort at both radio and television stations. We have audiences both on the air and online and both need to be satisfied with timely and credible news efforts. We also use social media as a source at times. In some cases today, more time is actually expended on social media than on traditional news reporting.

But as we have been made painfully aware of since the presidential campaign of 2016, not everything that is online or on social media is true. This is why we need to make sure that everything we use from social media is fully vetted and that we make sure our audience feels certain that anything we post is credible and accurate.

 ## Style Differences

While we deal with serious time constraints on the air for our stories, we have more latitude with what we put up on our station websites. For radio writers and reporters, we also have the opportunity to add video or photo stills to our efforts.

This means that we have the opportunity to add more details, more background and write the longer pieces that we often want to write. But we still want to maintain our 'electronic media' style so the stories have the same sound as they do on the air. That means you will want to follow all of the style points, legal considerations and stick to the conversational style that makes our form of communication so extremely effective.

Just because you are writing in long-form, you want to make sure not to revert to the style that you have been using to write term papers and reports during your college career. That is not broadcast style and while these stories are not actually being broadcasted, they still need to reflect the sound and attitude of your radio or TV station.

Just because you have more time and space to develop your story when creating it for online usage, you still need to write your story to only the length that the story demands. In other words, keep from writing and writing and writing. Write just what you need to write to make your story interesting, complete and engaging.

 ## Content Curation

The Internet is a wealth of information. Unfortunately quite a bit of what is put online is not true. Sometimes it is difficult to spot. The people who propagate 'Fake News' are pretty good at making their sites and posts look legitimate.

This means that if you are going to use information, content or quotes from online sources you need to make absolutely sure that they are 100-percent accurate. You need to know that the websites you are looking

Writing for Internet Usage

at are legitimate and from well-known, vetted sources. Personally, I only use information from sites maintained by other entities that I have personal knowledge of in the broadcast or entertainment world.

If you do use content from other types of sites, it will require some digging to find out the background of those who maintain the site and decide if they are credible. Obviously, you will likely not have time to do that while you are on deadline to get your stories ready for air, so a list of reliable source sites is something that you may want to work on when you have down time at the station or on your own off-time.

Even some of the most reliable sites allow others to post on them under their banner. The authors are usually listed and often have a link available where you can find their bios and other information that can speak to their credibility. Even if the bio looks professional, I will always do an additional Internet search to confirm the information it contains on the person. I also do not use any information from articles where the author is cited as 'anonymous' or where an Internet search does not come up with any additional biographical information on the person.

It is also a good idea, especially when finding content on sites you are not extremely familiar with, to double-check what you have found by doing a search for corroborating information. If you find discrepancies, you are going to need to hold back on including that information in your story until you can sort it out and determine what is correct before using it in your story.

There is also a very big benefit to you helping your station provide accurate and responsible content for the website. Most content curators will attribute back to the original site, which can be great promotion for your station's reputation as a reliable source of online news.

Spotting Fake News Sites

Sites that trade in false or inaccurate news have gotten pretty good at making themselves look legitimate. There are still some things to look for that might give them away. Things like strange domain names, domain extensions that you have never seen before or content written in all caps should be considered warning signs.

Many of these sites are known as aggregators. They don't do any reporting on their own. They take news stories from other sources and

153

Social and Multi-media News

then re-write them with sensational and often inflammatory headlines and without any real facts.

Facebook and Google have recently stepped up their efforts to block fake news sites from appearing in their feeds and searches or at least alert users that certain stories may contain 'disputed content'.

Another way to double-check a news story is to do an Internet search and see if any other media is reporting it. You just might find a number of stories pointing out that the exact story that you are checking is making the rounds and is totally false.

Proper Attribution

Attribution is important, both on the air and online. We talked about it extensively in Chapter 3 and essentially the same rules and conditions apply. And in the current climate, it becomes even more important.

When you use information you have gleaned from the wire services, you do not need to attribute. You can and it is not a bad idea, but you do not have to. Because your station pays for the license to use the different wire services, you have the right to do that. Some stations, however, do not want their stories to include attribution to the wire services. They prefer that their audience believes the station to be the source of the information, so this is something you will want to check out with each station you work for.

If you take information from a trusted website, then you should use attribution. When I do a story on the weekend box office results, I often use one of the big entertainment industry websites in conjunction with what I use from the wires. I will always say something like "xxx.com says . . ." somewhere in my story. It doesn't mean that I do not believe their information is not accurate, but since I did not gather it myself, it is important to let the audience know where it came from. In addition, in case another media outlet is reporting different results, it's a good idea to be able to source back to where your information came from.

Links to Other Media

To link or not to link. This is an issue that varies from station to station. Adding a link to a story to enable your readers to get more information

Writing for Internet Usage

on the story can be a good thing. But it does send a person off of your station's website and onto another unrelated site and many stations do not want this to happen.

Some stations prefer that you simply make sure to include all the pertinent information in your story with proper attribution, and be done with it. Others will allow you to reference the website within the body of the story, but not specify the exact link. Others will actually put a version of the story up on their website, social media or blog and have you direct the audience to the site for more information on the story.

How we tie social media, websites and on-air broadcasting is still relatively new and stations are always looking at new and better ways to do it. The key though is to keep the people coming back to the terrestrial broadcasts because that is still where the bulk of the income comes from.

Accuracy, Reliability and Responsibility

All of these considerations are crucial to being a responsible member of the news media. And they have never been more important than they are now with the increased scrutiny that the industry is under.

Checking and vetting content takes extra time and sometimes you don't have it, so you need to be able to work with the information you have and then go back and add the additional content as it is verified. There is no reason that an online story, or even an on-air story, cannot and should not be re-written as the facts change or new ones develop.

Shortcutting and not making every effort to ensure accuracy is never acceptable. While we often have to work fast and to very tight deadlines, you need to make sure that your stories come from reliable and vetted sources and that you have used attribution where it is required or suggested.

Your credibility and that of the station you work for is extremely important and hard to repair when damaged. The public has many outlets to find its information, both on-air and online, so it can be quick to dismiss a site where it finds the information is not reliable. By taking the time to make sure your information is accurate and well-sourced, you can help advance both your own reputation as a news professional as well as the reputation of the station.

Social and Multi-media News

 Points to Remember

- Even though you may be writing for the station's website, blog or social media, you still want to write in the same conversational style that you would use for stories that will be used on the air.

- When using any content found on the Internet, you should only source sites that you are personally familiar with and have previously vetted as reliable.

- Stations have varying policies on whether you can include website addresses in your stories. You should check with each station that you work for.

- If you don't have time to verify information from the web before using it in a story, don't use it. You can always add it later after you are sure that it is correct.

Exercises

1. Find five online sources for news that you consider credible. Explain why you are confident about the content on these sites.

2. Look at the following sites and determine if they should be considered as reliable resources. Explain your decision:

    - theonion.com
    - forbes.com
    - variety.com
    - infowars.com
    - buzzfeed.com
    - realnewsrightnow.com
    - dailycurrant.com
    - huffingtonpost.com
    - thelapine.com
    - tmz.com

Believability is your Credibility. Check your facts and fact check your checkers.
—Rhett Samuel Price – Former on-air talent at KABC-TV Channel 7 and KJLH, Los Angeles

Be honest in reporting. Unless it's an editorial don't include your opinion. It's better to produce a shorter story than a colorful, inaccurate, semi-truthful report that just sounds good.
—Brian Roberts – On Air Personality KYA San Francisco, Los Angeles' KUTE102, 1580 KDAY, MAGIC106, KZLA, KRLA, KEARTH101, WESTWOOD ONE RADIO NETWORK and CBS-FM

18 | Packaging for Multi-media

In this Chapter

- Online Audio and Video
- Use of Stills
- Podcasts
- RSS Feeds

Increasing Your Industry Vocabulary

- Podcast – A digital audio file that can be downloaded to a computer or mobile device via the Internet. Usually presented as a series
- RSS feeds – Rich Site Summary, also called Really Simple Syndication. A format that allows the delivery of web content that changes on a regular basis, such as news content
- Still – A photograph

To work in radio or television news you need to be a great writer and speaker. You need to be smart, quick and educated. And in today's world, you also need to be a good photographer, videographer and editor as well.

The business of radio and television has merged with the online and social media worlds and you need to be able to essentially do it all if you want to be successful.

Whether you are using your smartphone or more sophisticated equipment, your skills at creating and taking video are now an important part of your job.

We now are not only writing and filing our stories for use on the air, but also to websites, social media and podcasts.

Technology is changing fast and it is imperative for all of us to do our best to keep up with it and stay up to date. Radio and TV stations are doing the same and working to incorporate these changes into their programming.

Being savvy with this new technology and ways of delivering content on demand can be a very big factor in getting hired, not only for your first job but for subsequent jobs as you move to bigger markets.

Online Audio and Video

Digital audio and video seems to always be improving and is now to the point that it is easy to use and to include on websites and other online efforts by you and your station.

Websites and other online platforms allow radio stations to add video to their stories. This provides an exciting opportunity to direct the audience to our websites to actually see pictures from the stories that we have on the air. It's an advantage that should not be missed, but it does mean that radio reporters and writers need to be familiar with preparing and uploading these videos in order to make this happen.

There are still some considerations to think about. When it comes to video, the larger the file, the longer and more difficult it can be to download and play properly. We've probably all experienced trying to see a video and been forced to wait too long for it to load and buffer. Often, we simply give up before seeing it. People today are pretty impatient.

That means that you need to keep your videos relatively short. A great video is not good if it is not seen and a frustrated viewer may not come back to your site again after a bad experience.

Audio does not really suffer from this problem. Still, your audio should also be kept on the short side simply because people may not be willing to devote extensive amounts of time getting the information.

It is also still important to note that not everyone has the latest technology. Some people are viewing our efforts on older computers, tablets and smartphones. This is another reason to keep audio and video shorter so these older devices can handle them.

Use of Stills

There is a saying that a picture is worth a thousand words. And it is much quicker sometimes to take and upload a picture than to create a video. Today's smartphones take pictures of exceptional quality that is good enough for them to be used as online assets.

Not all pictures need to be edited, but most can benefit from some work. Photoshop is the most common picture editor out there and offers a great many tools to work with that are actually pretty simple to use.

While it is fine to make minor changes to a picture, such as cropping or lightening it, it is important that nothing is done to change the picture itself. You cannot add anything or remove something from the picture, even it if makes the picture fit your story better.

Knowing how to take digital pictures and work with Photoshop are skills that you should work to develop. Most colleges offer classes on both and although they might not be required to get your degree or certificate, they are well worth taking. Being able to state on your resume that you are proficient in these areas will be excellent assets when you start applying for jobs.

Podcasts

Podcasts are extremely simple to do, inexpensive and increasingly becoming a staple of radio and TV news efforts. They are also an excellent way to start working on your craft and developing an online presence as a reputable and professional broadcaster before you actually even get your first job.

Just like everything in our industry, podcasts are changing as technology changes. Podcasts originally started as audio-only presentations, but today they also can incorporate video as well.

Podcasts allow direct access to your listening audience. The audience that subscribes to your podcast does so because they are already interested in the topic you are talking about. Unlike a regular newscast, you do not have to worry about appealing to a broad audience.

Packaging for Multi-media

That's the good news. On the other side of the equation, because podcasts can easily be done at home with not much more than a microphone and access to the Internet, there is a lot of content available. That means there are a lot of podcasts out there, so quality matters if you want yours to stand out.

That means that not only does the writing and voicing have to be to industry standards, the podcast needs to sound like a professional endeavor. If you are doing a podcast on your own, think about creating a special, pre-produced introduction and outro that can also add information directing to your website or social media. Find a place where you can set up a proper sounding audio booth. There are several inexpensive table-top types on the market. Or you can go back to your childhood and build a sofa-cushion fort. No kidding, it works and a lot of us have done it before we were able to afford a real home studio! The best thing you can do for yourself is to invest in a good microphone. That's one of the keys to good sound. A professional-quality USB mic that you can use with your computer, laptop or tablet usually costs no more than $200.

The length of the podcast is important. Several studies have shown that after 22 minutes, the attention span of the average person starts to drop off. There are some very successful podcasts that are significantly longer, but 22 minutes is the recommended length for your podcast to be as effective as possible.

It is also possible to monetize your podcast. Because a podcast focuses on a specific topic or subject, it attracts an audience that has similar interests. That makes a successful podcast the ideal advertising vehicle for companies that are trying to reach that particular group of people. Advertising on a podcast can take the form of a billboard advertising that might be as simple as "This podcast sponsored by Joe's Pizza", all the way to including a full commercial somewhere in the program.

On the job, you may also find that contributing to a podcast may be part of your daily activities. Most stations allow you to repeat material that you have already used on the air. Others simply repackage recordings of material straight off the air.

Creating a podcast with a growing audience can be an excellent way of showing off your skills to a prospective employer. You will not only be able to demonstrate your skills with this type of technology, but also show that you can attract and keep an audience, something that is very important to any professional radio or TV station. If you have some impressive audience numbers, a savvy station manager is going to realize

Social and Multi-media News

that a good number of those people are likely to follow you over to your new job, because of course, you are going to talk about your new station in your podcast!

RSS Feeds

RSS stands for Rich Site Summary but some people prefer to call it Really Simple Syndication. It covers an entire group of web feed formats including blogs, news, audio, video and podcasts; pretty much any web-based content that changes frequently.

RSS allows for an automatic syndication of this material. Users are able to subscribe to RSS feeds that cover topics they are interested in. When new material becomes available, it is automatically downloaded to the user's device without the person having to manually recheck the original site.

Points to Remember

- It is not enough today to be good at writing, reporting and presenting the news. You also need to be proficient at editing video and photos.
- Social and multi-media skills are among the most sought after in the industry right now.
- Creating and hosting your own podcast is easy to do and a good way to start positioning yourself as a professional broadcaster.
- A good microphone is the best investment you can make in creating a quality podcast.

Exercises

1. For the following proposed website stories, look at shutterstock.com and select a picture that would be appropriate to include. You can cut and paste pictures from the site without opening or funding an account, but they will have the Shutterstock watermark on them, so they are not suitable for actual use:

Packaging for Multi-media

- A new freeway extension
- The start of the new model year of cars
- The latest iPhone
- The announcement of a new stadium being approved for your favorite sports team
- The latest diet fad
- The discovery of a new planet
- New user rules for Facebook
- A new law on texting while driving
- The start of summer
- The start of the new season of your favorite TV show

2. Most radio stations today are also podcasting. You can find a great many podcasts that are centered on news at this url: www.iheart.com/podcast/category/news-10/. Select one and listen to several episodes. Explain how this podcast compares to listening to the radio or television. How is it different and how is it the same? Do the same rules appear to apply to the podcast as they do to live newscasts? Is there something about the podcast that would convince you to subscribe?

> *Fact check! If information is wrong, no matter whose fault it may be, YOU as the reporter are the one that will lose credibility if facts are not correct.*
> —Samantha Stone – Traffic Reporter, Total Traffic & Weather Network/iHeart Media, Charlotte, North Carolina

Social Media as a News Source

19

In this Chapter

- The Role of Social Media
- Validating Social Media and Proper Vetting
- Legal Considerations
- Promotion Through Social Media

Increasing Your Industry Vocabulary

- Blog – An online element, usually on a website, that is regularly updated. Blogs are usually topic-specific. The name comes from the combination of web and log, as in journal

- Citizen journalist – A name given to a non-professional who documents news with a camcorder or smartphone and then publishes it on either a website or social media. The person may also seek to provide it to local radio or television stations for use on the air

- Interactivity – The process of two people or things working together and influencing each other

- Plagiarism – The act of taking someone else's words and passing them off as your own

- Social media – Computer-based technology that facilitates creating and sharing a variety of communication types such as ideas, information, conversations, discussion and career interests. Social media takes the form of virtual communities and networks

Social Media as a News Source

- User-generated content – Any kind of content such as video, audio or images that is created by non-professionals and is made available over the Internet to anyone who wants to use it. Also called UGC

- Vetting – The process of checking out information to make sure that it is reliable before using it or checking out a potential guest's credentials to make sure they are reputable before putting them on the air

Social media is a cultural phenomenon. Since its first origins in 1997 with a site called Six Degrees, it has made its way into nearly every aspect of our lives, both personal and professional. It started out as a fun tool for sharing ideas, information and conversations . . . and even for finding long lost friends. But it has turned into much more.

Today, many people feel like they cannot live without being active on social media. In fact, it has spawned several psychological conditions including Social Media Syndrome, which is where a person lives vicariously through others on social media, and Social Media Anxiety Disorder, which happens when overuse of social media interferes with a person's mental and physical health.

Using social media is no longer a choice; it is a necessity for both businesses and broadcasting professionals.

You will be using social media at your radio or TV station. To what extent depends on the decision of management at your station. However, it is a good idea for you to be well-versed in the most popular forms of social media and to start participating quickly as other platforms are developed and start to catch on. This is not only a selling tool when you begin looking for an internship or a job, but also will help you start developing a following as a news professional.

Social media can be a useful tool, especially when news is breaking and you are trying to find details quickly. At the same time, this information needs to be used carefully and not without verification.

Credibility is key in being considered a reliable source for news and information. As an employee of the radio or TV station, it is part of your responsibility to make sure that the material you use is verified before you use it. Hurrying to get something on the air is not an excuse for something making it to the air that is inaccurate.

You also need to make sure that any news information you share on your personal social media is accurate as well. Once you are working for a radio or TV station, your reputation and that of the station become

165

Social and Multi-media News

somewhat intertwined. That makes it imperative that the same tests for credibility and accuracy you use on the job you also apply to what you do on your personal social media.

The Role of Social Media

Social media has taken on a dual role in broadcasting. We've looked at how it's become a source of information on news stories but it is also a way for radio and TV stations to share news with listeners and get their feedback in return.

Due to the nature of social media, information is often disseminated much more quickly via a variety of platforms than it can be transmitted through the wire services. Social media can be accessed via law enforcement to get information out quickly about events or other issues pertaining to public safety. It is much quicker and more cost-effective than spending employee time trying to answer requests for information from reporters and news agencies over the phone. Witnesses or even victims can post information and be sure that it will be read quickly and shared thousands if not millions of times very quickly.

Social media is also a promotional tool for individuals as well as radio and TV stations and can be a valuable asset to their news efforts. It allows stations to let followers know about stories that are coming up on traditional channels or to provide additional information on stories that are being aired. Individual on-air talent can use it to promote the stories that they are working on.

Due to the fact that anyone can post on social media, it has become a home for what are called 'citizen journalists'. These are individuals who primarily use their smartphones or other mobile devices to collect video and/or audio from the scenes of news. They likely do not have any actual journalistic training or experience. They may be reliable or they may be creating and spreading phony news or information. The material that they generate and post is referred to as user-generated content.

Social media is also a way for on-air talent to self-promote and at many stations, this is a requirement. News anchors and reporters are often required to maintain a professional Facebook page along with a presence on other social media sites and post information related to their station-related work. They may also be asked to maintain a blog as well. In addition,

166

Social Media as a News Source

some stations expect on-air talent to also use Twitter to promote stories they are working on or will be presenting and also to interact with listeners about those stories.

Validating Social Media and Proper Vetting

Social media is a valuable tool, but it is one that needs to be used with caution. Not everything that appears on social media is from a reliable source or is posted with any kind of verification. Information that appears on social media is often repeated or shared many times without any further checking on its accuracy.

Just the same as we should do with any information that we get, information found on social media should not be used in your stories or on the air unless it is vetted by another reliable source. You might think of such information as a 'tip' that will lead you to verified details that you can feel confident about using.

There is no set way to do this. You can feel confident about a story that comes down on the wire services. The major services like AP or Reuters perform vetting on their stories before transmitting them. It is in their best interest to make sure that the information they send down the wires is accurate in order to maintain their reputation as a reliable news source. But, the information that is coming down is being written or collected by humans and they can make mistakes. If you have any doubt, you should make a phone call to the agency involved in the story if possible or look for reliable corroborating information from an additional source before using the material in your story or putting it on the air.

You can also choose to use attribution in your story as we discussed in Chapter 3. Using attribution does not protect you, though, if the information you use is inaccurate. It simply lets your audience know the origin of the information. If the information is incorrect, it will still reflect on your reputation and that of the station and can damage its credibility.

Information from sites that belong to law enforcement, government agencies or other organizations is generally considered to be reliable. You still need to be careful when using information from individual companies or businesses. Articles or information posted on their websites and social media sites may look like news, but can simply be an ad for something

167

Social and Multi-media News

they are involved in or are promoting. Take your time and understand what you are using before putting it into your story.

Legal Considerations

When information is posted on a company's website, such as CNN or ESPN, it is there for the use of viewers of the site. It is not there for news writers to use as part of their station's newscasts. Upon posting the material, it is copyrighted to that organization. It's called an 'implied copyright'. Unless your station has some sort of agreement with that company to use the information, you cannot legally do so.

This does not only apply to using the material in a story that will be read on air or recorded for later use. Copying that story for inclusion on the station's website or social media will constitute plagiarism and a violation of copyright law.

When working with online usage, some stations will allow you to write a short introduction to such articles and then provide a link to the story on its original site. This is not the best practice as it takes a viewer away from the station's site and onto the site of another, with no guarantee that they will return to the site belonging to the station.

When your station subscribes to a wire service, such as AP or Reuters, that subscription gives you, as an employee of that station, the right to use the information verbatim and without any attribution.

But when you use information found on social media, there is no real copyright protection for the author of that material. That means there is no copyright violation to be concerned with. But there is something much more important to consider. If that information is false, and you use it in a story that airs on your station, your station is in effect vouching for the fact that the information is accurate. If it is not, then you and your station could be held liable for damages or defamation arising from the airing or dissemination of those details on your station, its websites or on social media.

Promotion Through Social Media

News moves fast, very fast. A station can create a well-produced promo to let viewers or listeners know about a story that will air later the same day or

168

even the next day if it is one that the crew has been working on. But social media allows a station to promote a story that may have just come in or is breaking. The station may put the entire story on its social media pages or use them to tease back to an upcoming newscast on the air.

Stations not only promote themselves on social media, but may also require on-air personalities to promote themselves as representatives of the station. Others may want reporters and news anchors to maintain an active dialogue throughout the day with followers as another way of promoting and developing listener loyalty.

Points to Remember

● Media professionals are expected to be active on social media. A good presentation and an impressive number of followers can all be good selling points when you are looking for a job.

● Law enforcement and many other official agencies are using social media to not only reach the public but also to inform the media about breaking and emergency situations.

● Just as anything else we find on the Internet, any information found on social media needs to be fully vetted before using it as a tip or in a story.

● It is likely that social media activity will be part of your job description as a radio or TV news writer, reporter or anchor.

Exercises

1. There are many very well-document and high-profile cases of plagiarism. Research and write a story about one of the following cases by doing the required Google search:

   ● Kenny Florian Fox Sports plagiarism

   ● Lisa Rein Washington Post plagiarism

   ● Matthew Whitaker Arizona State University plagiarism

   ● Amy Schumer jokes plagiarism

   ● Nick Cavell Wired plagiarism

Social and Multi-media News

You will need to make sure that you are using a reputable website for your research. Include a paragraph in your report on how you have vetted the site to make sure that its information is credible.

2. Choose a topic for a blog and write a sample post. Your post should be around 300 words. Use shutterstock.com to select an appropriate image to include with your post.

Remember this is a business first – get our business degree and minor in journalism, communications, etc.
—Gary Leone – Sr. Executive Producer
Emeritus Shadow Traffic/Metro
Networks, Philadelphia

PART

VI

Presenting the News

IxMaster/shutterstock.com

The Right Attitude and Approach

20

In this Chapter

- Understanding the Story
- The Delivery
- Attitude Changes During the Newscast

Increase Your Industry Vocabulary

- Cold read – The act of reading a story on the air without first reading or rehearsing it
- One-on-one delivery – Reading the story in the way that it would sound if you were simply talking to someone else
- Attitude – The overall feel that you give a story with your voice, pace and expression

A good script is only the first step. Your on-air presentation can make or break a story.

No one wants to be read to or talked at. Your job is to present the story as if you are simply telling someone what is going on. That you have the information and you are simply sharing it with the other person.

To make that real, your demeanor needs to match the tone and topic of the story to make that believable.

Presenting the News

Understanding the Story

As a reporter, this is easy because you originated the story. As an anchor, you need to learn to be a quick read. Sometimes you don't even see the copy before you are about to read it on the air.

It's not just about the words. It's the topic of the story that you need to very quickly analyze and present to your audience with the appropriate style for the content. Anything less and people are not going to believe that you know anything about the story at all. And there goes your credibility.

When many of us started, we were told not to show any emotion on the air. That worked when newscasters and reporters were truly announcers. But it does not work with today's one-on-one delivery. Obviously, we don't mean laughing hysterically or sobbing or crying on the air. But showing emotion on your face and letting it come through in your voice is perfectly acceptable.

For example, if you have a negative or sad story, you certainly would not do it with a smile on your face or an upbeat sound in your voice. That would be totally inappropriate. But if you have a funny story, an entertainment story or something else light, then it is correct to smile, sound positive or even laugh a little. We need to have the proper tone and the proper inflections to match the words in the script.

The Delivery

As we said, no one wants to be read to or talked at. We want to be talked to. The key to make that work is to develop a one-on-one delivery. Even though there may be millions of people listening or watching, you need to trick yourself into believing that there is only one person out there.

This person is not just anyone. When you start out, this needs to be someone that you feel safe with, someone who will not chastise you if you make a mistake.

There are several tricks you can use to help develop this ability. Once you have selected your person, you have to learn to convince yourself that they are the only person out there listening or watching. If you are on the radio or a reporter, you may want to put a picture of that person where you can see it when you are on the air. Another idea is to bring in a stuffed

174

The Right Attitude and Approach

animal that you can talk to. I know this might sound silly. Many of my students have told me it does. Until they get so frustrated with their on-air performance and they decide they have nothing to lose by giving it a try. That's when they find out, like I did, that it works!

My very first job was on the radio as a disc jockey. I vividly remember how scared I was on my first night. I was just 19 and had just finished 'DJ School'. Somehow I had landed my first job just outside of Los Angeles, the number two market in the nation.

The jock who was going off the air before me could tell I was petrified. He graciously stayed with me for about an hour, even though it was midnight, both as moral support and to help me remember everything that I had learned but suddenly forgotten.

When he finally did have to leave, he drew me a little stick-figure man, tacked the drawing up behind the microphone and told me "to talk to him and you will be all right. He is your friend."

I thought, as you might be thinking right now, "Yeah right, that will really work." Well, after a few more disastrous breaks, I thought "what did I have to lose" and started talking to this skinny little figure each time I opened the mic.

Believe it or not, it did work. I focused on just talking to him and almost immediately I was no longer so scared. By the end of the night, I had found a way to pretend that it was just him and me and that we were friends.

After a while, you won't need whatever visual aid you decide to use. You will have developed this skill and will be able to use it without even thinking about it.

By the way, I still have that little stick-figure drawing. I haven't needed him for a great many years, but he is a great reminder of what it was like to be a beginner.

Sound confident. That is so important. If you hesitate or sound unsure of yourself, once again, your audience is not going to believe you know what you are talking about. "Loud and proud" is an old broadcasting slogan. Maybe you don't need to say it so loudly, but enunciate everything clearly, keep your volume up and present your script with confidence.

Use your hands! Most people talk with their hands. We use our hands when we talk to enhance or underscore what we are saying. So why wouldn't you also use them when you are on the air? After all, we are

Presenting the News

trying to sound conversational and similar to how we sound when we are just talking to a friend.

For radio, you need to make sure that when you gesture you don't hit anything. That means you can't pound on the table to make a point and you need to be aware of the mic boom, which is probably rather close to you. For TV, you need to keep your gestures pretty much in front of you so that your hands don't go out of the frame on a close shot or in front of your co-anchor in a wide shot. And for both, ladies, make sure you are not wearing bracelets that jingle because the mic will pick them up.

Gesturing on TV should be minimal and not constant throughout the newscast. So what do you do with your hands the rest of the time? The answer is . . . hold a pen. A pen is not only a good thing to use to keep one hand busy, but it also can be useful in case, for some reason, you need to write something down. It also is an appropriate prop for a newscaster and subliminally makes the listener think that you had a hand in writing the news you are presenting.

If you watch TV news anchors, you will also notice that they have a copy of the script in front of them on the desk. There is nothing wrong with holding it or stacking it even though you will be reading off the tele-prompter. It's there in case the teleprompter goes out, which very, very rarely happens, but it can and since you will be on the air live, it doesn't hurt to be safe!

Attitude Changes During the Newscast

Any newscast is made up of a variety of stories. That means you may need to adjust your approach to each story as you make your way through the cast.

Doing this can involve a number of things:

- Changing your inflection and attitude as you go from one to the next, depending on the topic of the story.

- Changing your pace, slowing down on a serious story and speeding up just a bit on a lighter or humorous story.

- For TV, you may want to lean in on the desk a bit on a more serious story.

The Right Attitude and Approach

You have a lot to think about and be aware of when you are on the air, whether it is on radio or TV. With all of that, you still need to appear confident, professional and most of all approachable and friendly. You want your viewers and listeners to feel comfortable with you, believe you and consider you as a trustworthy friend.

Points to Remember

- Your pace, tone and inflections need to match the topic of the story you are reading.
- It is ok to show some emotion when you are on the air.
- You need to develop the ability to sound as if you are talking to one person, not millions.
- Use your hands when you talk. It will make you sound more conversational.

Exercises

1. Using this newscast line-up, what kind of attitude would you expect to present with each story? Use one or two words to describe the proper demeanor for each story:
   - A story about a new law by the president
   - A story about a missing person
   - A story about a bank robbery
   - A story about the death of a city councilman
   - A story about the opening of a new park
   - A story about the birth of a new giraffe at the zoo

2. Record your first read of the following story. As you read it, picture who you might actually talk to about the subject of the story. Listen to your recording and see if it sounds like you are just telling the story to one person. What do you need to do to make it more conversational?

177

Make those adjustments and read and record it again. Turn in your list of changes that you made between versions one and two along with both recordings:

Records are coming back. Vinyl records started disappearing in the 1990s as CDs became popular. But now records have gained a whole new fan base. Younger people are discovering vinyl and turntables and people who grew up listening to records are finding they prefer their sound over music on digital downloads. Now CD and digital sales are starting to decline as a result of the popularity of Spotify and Pandora. At the same time, Nielsen Music says the sale of records has grown from less than 1-million a year in 2005 to nearly 13-million albums in 2016.

The first comment my broadcasting teacher said on the first day of class was "Your job is to create filler in between the commercials". His second, "You will never enjoy the creative freedom you have in college ever again. Enjoy it while it lasts". I never forgot either and truer words were never spoken.
—Michael Weinstein – Photo Journalist at Helicopters Inc., St. Louis, Missouri; Former Newswriter at CBS Radio News, Former Traffic Reporter at Total Traffic Network

Looking Like a Pro

21

In this Chapter

- Professionalism
- Looking the Part
- Personal Choices

Increasing Your Industry Vocabulary

- Camera-ready – Being ready to go in front of the cameras. Applies to clothing, but can also pertain to hair and make-up
- Internship – An opportunity to work at a radio station, TV station, studio, etc., in order to gain experience and make contacts. Generally, interns are not paid, but receive college credit
- Professionalism – Acting and looking like a professional. This applies to speech, attitude and appearance

One of the hardest things when you are just starting out in any field is being taken seriously. You know you can do the job, you just need to get everyone else to believe you can.

As they say "You never get a second chance to make a great first impression" and it is very true. Research shows that people make a decision about you in only about seven seconds. You are jumping into a television or radio station full of professionals. Hopefully you've done at least

179

Presenting the News

one, and perhaps several, internships, so you have an idea of how things work. But it still can be very intimidating.

On the subject of internships, they are an essential part of getting into the broadcast news business. A lot of stations will not even consider hiring someone who has not done at least one internship. Many students put off doing their internships because they see it as having to work for free. While paid internships are rare, what you don't get in minimum wage pay, you make up several times over in experience, contacts and confidence. You'll have a chance to see what working at a radio or TV station is really like and that will go a long way in helping you land your first job.

If you look and act like you belong, then you will feel more like you do and that will affect not only your attitude and comfort-level, but your performance as well.

Professionalism

Professionalism is defined as the conduct and qualities that characterize or mark a profession or a professional person. It means you need to look and act like a pro to be taken seriously as one.

Much of doing this is really common sense. It includes things like:

- Being on time
- Not using your cellphone at work for calls, texting, games or anything else unless you are at lunch or on a break
- Not divulging work-related information on social media or elsewhere
- Refraining from gossiping about others either at work or on your own time
- Remembering people's names

This doesn't mean you shouldn't enjoy your time at work and have fun while you are doing your job. You just need to remember that there is work to be done and that nothing should get in the way of you doing your part properly and on time.

Looking the Part

Your decisions on hair, make-up and clothes will change throughout your career and have a lot to do with the market you are working in. You will find some parts of the country are more conservative and expect that to be reflected by the news professionals they watch on television. Other parts of the country are more trendy.

For radio, obviously these choices are not as crucial as they are for television, but they still are very important. You want to look like you belong.

Often people trying to get into radio overdress when they go into the interview and during their first few days on the job. Radio is a rather casual medium and that should be your guideline in how you dress. 'Nice casual' is the standard. Guys do not need to wear a suit and tie and ladies do not need to wear a dress. On the other hand, jeans, t-shirts, tennis shoes and such are not recommended when you are trying to make that all important first impression.

Once you are working at the station, you can relax your dress code to match what the other people there are wearing. Once again, exactly what that is will depend on what part of the country you are located in. Some areas, like Los Angeles, are very casual. Others may be more formal. Once you are at the station, you will be able to figure out just how casual is acceptable.

For television, you want to be 'camera-ready' when you go in for an interview. That means dressing as if you were going to be on the air that very day. This can be a little bit deceiving sometimes. Obviously, you should be watching the station you want to be on to get an idea of what the people on the air are wearing. But for your initial introduction to the station, you may want to ramp up your look a little bit more. That might mean a suit coat over a sports jacket for the guys and a dress or top with sleeves for the girls.

Once again, after you are hired, you can dress a bit more casual if that is the trend at the station.

It's always a very good idea to avoid wearing anything green. If you happen to have to work with a green screen, any green clothing that you might be wearing will seem to disappear. You may also want to avoid anything with a small pattern on it as these tiny images can sometimes seem to almost be moving on camera.

Personal Choices

Sometimes your personal choices and your professional choices don't exactly match. And you need to consider this when deciding on whether or not to do something. This applies to things like extreme hair coloring or styling choices, piercings and tattoos.

While we all have a right to express ourselves, certain things may not be as widely accepted as others and certain areas may be more liberal about these things than others.

This is truly something that you need to think about, especially if what you are considering doing is something that you cannot remove or at least cover up when you need to. It would be a shame if a personal choice was to cost you your first job and it certainly could, especially in television. You need to keep in mind that in such a position, your audience will contain people of all ages and your look has to be acceptable to all groups. You also are representing the image of the station with every choice you make about your personal appearance and presentation.

Points to Remember

- It's important to make a good first impression and you only have about seven seconds to do it.
- If you want to be accepted as a professional, you need to look and act like one.
- Internships are a great way to gain an understanding of what to expect in the workplace.
- You need to carefully consider getting things like tattoos and piercings that may be difficult to hide or cover up if you have to.

Exercises

1. Watch your local news station and see what the on-air talent is wearing. Do they look professional? Look through several online catalogs and create a collection of at least five 'looks' that you think would work for you as a television news professional.

Looking Like a Pro

2. Select a local radio or television station, find out who handles its internship program and interview that person. You want to find out, among other things, what the requirements are for applying, what skills they are looking for and what kind of tasks interns do at the station. Write your findings in a report using the conversational newswriting style that we have been working on in this course.

> *The story is the star, not the reporter. It's not about you. It's about what your audience wants and needs to know.*
> —Alan Mendelson – former Radio, TV, print and Internet Reporter, now Advertising Company Owner

PART VII

Becoming a Pro

Forest Run/shutterstock.com

22 | The Life of a News Professional

In this Chapter

- On-call and 24/7 Schedules
- Stress and Emotions
- Travel and Relocating
- Family Life

News Never Sleeps. And sometimes it feels like those of us in the industry don't either! Crazy schedules and a high level of stress are things that need to be understood and considered by anyone thinking about going into this business. It definitely will have an impact on your life and your family. If you are looking for a nine-to-five that will get you home for dinner on time every evening, then broadcasting is not for you. But if you like never knowing exactly what is going to happen each day when you go to work, then it sounds like you have found your calling!

On-call and 24/7 Schedules

The news business is not a normal job. It's not a five-day-a-week job. It doesn't care about holidays . . . not even Thanksgiving or Christmas. And this is something you have to be prepared for.

In radio, you are likely to start on the overnight shift. That will be something like midnight to five or six in the morning. And perhaps some shifts on the weekend. In television, it's also probably going to be a

187

Becoming a Pro

weekend shift. It's a foot in the door and that's what counts, but sometimes it can be a bit difficult to deal with.

You may also find yourself on-call. That means you could be offered additional hours at the station or you may not have any regularly scheduled hours at all and work only when needed to cover for someone who is out sick or otherwise unexpectedly unable to make their shift, or during breaking news or another big news event when everyone is needed to pitch in. It means that the station expects you to be available when it needs you. And these call-ins often come with very little advance notice.

This can be a bit tricky if you are going to school or have another job to help pay the bills. But, turning down call-ins from the station will result in the station calling you less and less and perhaps ultimately not at all. Obviously, the more often you are at the station, the more experience you will get and the more management will be able to see you. Hopefully, at some point, the station will offer you more of a part-time or a full-time position. That's what you want so you will have to keep yourself available as much as possible if you are on call.

Even once you are full-time, you are always on-call when you work in news. If something big happens, you will probably be called in, even if it means that you work more than 40 hours in that week. You may even end up working more than eight hours in a day. When breaking news happens, the station usually needs all hands on deck to handle the coverage. And if you are part of the station, you will *want* to be there. Covering breaking news is fast-paced and exhausting, but exciting and exhilarating at the same time.

Stress and Emotions

Dealing with the news is stressful all by itself. Dealing with a schedule with odd hours or being on-call can be stressful as well.

When you report or anchor the news, you are dealing with a lot of negativity. And you often know more details about the stories than what you put on the air. Often, they are not pleasant details.

Because you are a professional, you probably will tend to keep a lot of this to yourself. You won't tell others in your personal life because you won't want to share things that may cause them to worry about you. Most of us want to keep this kind of information from invading our family lives.

The Life of a News Professional

It is really important that you have an outlet for all of this. We often get very busy with everyday living and forget to take time out for ourselves. Not making your life as balanced as possible can affect your on-air performance in a negative way and your health as well, so find ways to take a break and do something for yourself with friends and family at least once a week.

Travel and Relocating

Depending on what part of the country you are in, you may have to relocate in order to get your start in the industry. It is very difficult, if not impossible, to start in a major market such as Los Angeles or New York. You need to target smaller markets where your current skills will match the skills of the people already working there. You do not want to introduce yourself to a market before your skills are ready for that market.

This means that you are probably going to need to move. And perhaps move several times before you make it to the market where you really want to be. Each step in this process will be a learning experience and give you a chance to become an even better broadcaster.

Sometimes, you may be able to negotiate all or part of your moving expenses as part of your deal with your new station. This may include your transportation to the new location, the moving of your furniture and other belongings and a hotel room or corporate housing to stay in while you find an apartment or home to rent.

Not everyone gets their start in a small market. The more you do at your college radio or television station, the more internships you do, the better your chances of starting out at a larger station. You want to take every opportunity that is offered to you and seek out as many other chances as possible to continue improving your skills.

Family Life

Moving is never easy and for many people in the news industry it is a way of life, especially in the early years of their careers. This is certainly something you will want to discuss with your significant other because moving will not only affect your life but also that of the other members of your immediate family.

Becoming a Pro

It takes a special person to be the partner of someone in this industry. There are a lot of wonderful opportunities that come with the profession, not just for you but that will also be extended to your significant other, but it does come with a lot of give-and-take on the part of that other person.

Working as a news anchor or reporter is certainly not an average life, but as challenging as it can be it is also fantastic. You will get to go and do and see things that are rarely available to the general public. You will meet people that many just dream of meeting. You will have the chance to educate, entertain and help thousands or even millions of people over your career. All of this comes with a price, but most of us think it is well worth it.

Points to Remember

- Working in broadcast news takes a real commitment because of the crazy hours and schedules you will be dealing with, especially when you are starting out.
- You may have to move to get started in the business.
- It's important to take time out for yourself each week even when there doesn't seem to be any time to do it.

Exercises

1. Make a list of what is important to you in terms of your lifestyle and contrast that with what you consider the key reasons are for wanting to become a news professional. Look at things like future family plans, locations where you would like to live, outside activities that you enjoy, etc. Once you complete this assignment, you may have a better idea of whether you feel the sacrifices are worth the rewards of getting into this industry.

2. There are certain personality traits that tend to make a good broadcaster. See how you score by ranking the following traits one to ten . . . one being 'not so good' and ten being 'fantastic'.

   - Are you a good communicator?
   - Are you curious?

The Life of a News Professional

- Can you deal with a variety of different kinds of people?
- Are you multi-skilled?
- Are you willing to learn new things?
- Can you handle pressure and deadlines?
- Are you a team player?
- Are you able to work without direct supervision?
- Are you detail-oriented?
- Are you able to handle last-minute changes?

> *As a journalist, you will be invited to lots of fancy parties. You will have access to wonderful people, places and things. You will get free tickets to all sorts of events. Just remember, no one is giving you all that stuff because of your good looks and charm. They will want something in return. Don't fall for it. Don't be used.*
>
> —Roger Aldi – former News Director
> at KHJ, KRLA, KPOL and KDAY

23 | Creating and Marketing Your Demo

In this Chapter

- Cover Letters and Resumes
- Creating Material
- Websites
- Internet Presence
- Branding and Marketing

You might feel like you are somewhat between a rock and a hard place when it comes to preparing the materials that you are going to need to get your first job. You haven't worked yet so you may not have much that really demonstrates your abilities. But you still need a way to prove to a prospective station that you have the skills that they are looking for.

There really are a lot of ways that you can make yourself look like a broadcast professional and it isn't really as hard as you might think it is.

As we mentioned in Chapter 21, an internship is one of the best ways to prepare yourself for entering the job market. But even to land an internship, you will need to prepare some professional-level marketing materials.

Cover Letters and Resumes

These two things are usually the first items that will represent you to a prospective employer so you need to put some thought into them and do them with care.

Creating and Marketing Your Demo

Many people are confused about the difference between the two. They actually each serve very different purposes. The cover letter is going to be your introduction. It will tell the reader why they are getting your package, what it includes and a little bit about you. You don't want to tell them all about yourself; save most of that for your resume and your interview. The cover letter will also state what you would like to have happen next. If you are hoping for an interview, then go ahead and say that. If you would like to talk on the phone, then put that request in the letter. And always include your cellphone number and email address on everything you send when you are pursuing a position.

The resume builds on the cover letter. This is where you spell out all your qualifications. You may not think you have anything that a radio or television station will be interested in, or if you do, that they are important enough to matter. But I bet you really do. While you may not have tremendous skills yet as a broadcaster, you probably have skills that a station manager would be interested in. Have you held down a job with special responsibilities? Have you worked at the same job for more than six months? Has your college career included extra-curricular activities? Have you mastered social media? All of these things count to the impression that you are trying to make.

On your resume, you will want to have at least the following sections:

- Education
- Related Work Experience
- Work History
- Skills and Qualifications

You may also want the following sections:

- Goals
- Award and Achievements

And of course, you want to list your contact information including your cellphone and your email address.

Your resume should be no more than one page in length. That's pretty easy to do if you keep your items and descriptions short and to the point.

193

Becoming a Pro

You don't want to give away all the details. You need to save those for the interview which we will look at in Chapter 24.

It is also extremely important that both your resume and cover letter are neat and look professional and that everything is spelled correctly. Mistakes will give your prospective employer an unfavorable impression of you and could prevent you from even getting an interview. You want your materials to represent you as the kind of person the station would want to bring on staff.

Creating Material

Throughout your college career, you need to be collecting material that can be used when you get ready to start looking for that first job. This material can be from broadcasts on the campus radio or television station or from assignments that you have done for your classes that you are particularly proud of.

The people you will be sending your package to understand that you are a beginner, but they are still looking for a polished performance so you only want to submit your very best work.

You can also create some materials for your demo reel if you don't have anything. The one thing to remember is never to use real station call letters, names or anything else that would give the impression that you actually worked for those stations. Your campus station's identifiers are fine, but don't use any from a professional station. You don't want the person reviewing your materials to think that you are trying to get credit for something that you didn't do.

Whatever you put together, keep it short. Your radio demo should be no more than one-minute and 30-seconds. Your TV demo should be no longer than five minutes. Just like with that first impression when it comes to how you look, you don't get much longer to impress people with your skills.

Websites

You need a website. Everyone working as a professional does. It does not have to be elaborate or expensive. There are many online sites that will let you build one for free and host it at a relatively small cost.

A website is a chance to present yourself and your accomplishments. You can also post your demos on it and direct prospective employers to it as an easy way for them to hear and see your work.

Just like with everything that you do publicly, you need to keep your website professional. It can be fun, colorful and entertaining, but you need to keep in mind that it is actually a marketing tool so you will want to avoid putting a lot of the personal material on it.

Internet Presence

Social media is no longer just for the fun of it. It is essential for just about everyone in any profession. It is especially important for anyone involved in media because we actually now use it as part of our jobs.

Facebook, Twitter and LinkedIn are must-haves. Instagram is also important but not essential to your professional endeavors. Of them all, LinkedIn is the most important to your job search. A great many companies who are looking for candidates for jobs use LinkedIn so it's important to start building your network as soon as possible.

It's no revelation that you need to be careful about what you put on social media. No matter how you set your privacy settings, companies that do background checks can still get in and see what you have posted and even what you have deleted.

It's not uncommon for a company to take a look at your social media even before calling you in for a first interview. If they see something they don't like, they probably will not spend the time getting to know you beyond that.

Branding and Marketing

What is your brand? Basically that means how do you want to show yourself to the market? It's a difficult and important question and takes quite a bit of thought. You start with your desired job. Reporter, anchor, radio, television? That's the easy part. Then you need to figure out how your personality figures into the equation. Are you serious, investigative, humorous? How will that connect with your desired job and how you present yourself? What makes you special and different from everyone else out there?

Becoming a Pro

Once you have this figured out, you may want to have a logo created. It does not have to be elaborate. It can just be a specific script of your name in a font that conveys your personality. You will want to use this logo across everything you do online and include it on your personal business cards as well.

Business cards are another small thing that can have a big impact in your efforts to look professional. All they really need to have on them is your name and contact information. You might want to list the areas of the industry that you are proficient in or you could put the names of some of the programs that you are skilled in such as ProTools or Final Cut Pro.

Mainly, your business cards are an easy way to give someone your contact information, so be sure to include your cellphone number, email and info on all of your social media accounts.

One thing that I started doing years ago was to include my signature color, hot pink, into all of my branding and marketing. It is a key color in my logo and also appears on my website and my social media. Not a lot of it, just a little, but it is consistent. Why hot pink? Well, first I just really like the color, but I also think it conveys the message that although I do mostly serious news, I also have a playful side that transcends into the other areas of the industry that I'm involved in.

Points to Remember

- Your cover letter and resume need to look professional, be free of errors and be no more than one page each.

- Work you have done at your college radio or TV station can be used on your demo reel.

- You need to create a website aimed at your professional goals.

- It's important to maintain an active social media presence on the most popular platforms.

- You should develop a branding strategy and include it on all of your materials and social media efforts.

Creating and Marketing Your Demo

Exercises

1. Create a resume and a matching cover letter to use in applying for your first job. Each should be no more than one page in length. Use your cover letter to show your conversational style of writing. Your resume should highlight your qualifications for the job you are hoping to get.

2. Write a bullet-point list to use to start creating your brand. Include the following items:

   - Words that describe you as a news professional
   - Colors that you want to use on your website, logo and business cards
   - Images that you think will help to illustrate your brand
   - Slogans or statements that could be used to help define your style or philosophy as a media professional

     > *Strive for honesty in all that you do. Don't be afraid to say you don't have the answer – but you'll find it. Aim to be someone people will trust even if you are giving them news they don't want to hear.*
     >
     > —Nichole Davis – Traffic Reporter, WBZ-AM, Boston

24 | News Tests and Interviews

 In this Chapter

- Preparing for the Interview
- Being a Successful Interviewee
- News Tests
- Follow-up

Radio and television stations rarely make quick decisions about who to hire especially when they are hiring someone new to the industry. So be prepared to spend some very nervous days hoping that you are about to get your first important break.

You can help the process along, though, by working proactively to land the job. And that is what we are going to discuss in this chapter.

 Preparing for the Interview

If you've been called in for an interview, congratulations! It means the materials you have already provided your prospective employer have impressed them to the point that they want to meet you. Now you have to continue to impress in person.

Before the interview, you need to do some more research. You likely did some before you applied in order to make sure that your resume, demo and other materials were in line with how the station presents itself. But now you need to expand your information. You need to be prepared to talk

News Tests and Interviews

with someone about the station, its programming and how you are ready to become a part of it.

Obviously, you are going to be nervous, so that makes it especially important to be prepared. There are many ways to do this. Check out the station's website, listen or watch the station so you know about any current specials or promotions, look at what some of the station's personalities are posting on social media.

Most importantly, think about you and the station. You'll need to be ready to talk about how you will fit in and what you can bring to the station. Think about your skills and areas where you think you would be an asset.

A word of caution though: Keep from criticizing any area of the station, personalities or programming. While you may be ready to join the station as a professional, you aren't ready to pass judgment on any part of the industry just yet.

You will have to give your opinion if asked. You can do it without coming off incorrectly by first giving some praise to what the station is currently doing in that area and then making your suggestion. This way you avoid giving the impression that you are there to save the world and that you have all the answers!

Being a Successful Interviewee

Think of your interview as an audition. That means you need to be on your game from the time you get to the station to the time that you leave it.

A student of mine once lost a job before he even got into the interview by not understanding that. This was a job that I had recommended him for at the same station where I was working. Management was pretty much sold on him after reviewing his materials and hearing me sing his praises.

He had gotten there on time and was waiting in the lobby. The News Director came out to get him and on the way back to her office, she asked him how the drive had been. She knew from his resume that he had quite a long drive from his home to the station. Without missing a beat, he said the trip had been very long and he didn't know how people did it every day.

That was pretty much the end of the interview. They talked for a short time, he got a quick tour of the studio and that was it. He did not get the

199

Becoming a Pro

job. A few days later when he and I talked about it, I explained to him how that one comment had lost it for him. He proclaimed that was not fair, that the interview had not 'officially' started since they were not in her office yet when he made the comment. Wrong, the interview starts at the front door of the station.

A good interview is a conversation, not an interrogation. That means that information should be going both ways. If you only answer the questions asked of you, then that is all the interviewer will ever learn about you. Of course, you need to let them lead the conversation, but it's important to add information about yourself wherever appropriate.

Another important key is to ask some questions yourself. You can start to have rapport immediately with the person interviewing you by asking some questions about them . . . things like how they got started in the industry and what they like most about their job at this particular station. It is easier to hire someone if you like them. Help the person who is interviewing you like you by letting them see you as a person.

Finally, you should ask when they plan to make a decision on who they are going to hire. This will give you some guidance on how to plan your follow-up, which we will discuss later in this chapter.

News Tests

By this point in the process, you have already provided the station with your demo and they have undoubtedly already listened or viewed it. But the process of your proving yourself may not be over yet.

Be prepared at your interview to have another opportunity to show your abilities and your skills. It's no secret that the demo you submitted may not have been your first take. Just like you, prospective employers are familiar with how easy it is to edit and enhance audio or video, so you may be asked to prove yourself in real time.

This might mean going into the audio booth with a script and being asked to record it. You're not just being asked to do a good job on the voicing but to do it in a very short amount of time to prove you can do the job live on the air. For television, you might be asked to go on set, sit at the anchor desk and read off the teleprompter in a sample newscast. Employers are looking for people who are ready to work the moment they are hired and you need to be able to prove that you are ready. As a news

News Tests and Interviews

writer for either radio or television, you may be asked to sit down at a computer and write a newscast by going through the wire service, selecting stories and rewriting the copy. This means you will have to have a quick study on the news platform that the station is using and complete that newscast about as quickly as you would be expected to do on the job.

Follow-up

Once you have gone through all the preliminaries and the interview itself, you do not want to drop the ball. You need to do a good job of following up.

Within 24 hours of your interview, you need to send an email to the person you met with thanking them for the opportunity and for their time. This is also a good time to add any additional information about yourself that you forgot to mention during the interview and suddenly remembered on the way home. You should also mention how much you want the job.

Too often we actually fail to ask for what we want. We hope that the other person will already know that or pick up on the hints that we are sending. While obviously the person who interviewed you knows you want the job, making that statement will make you stand out from the others who were interviewed.

Employers want to hire a person who wants the job they are offering. Not just any job, because they need a job, but that specific job. Stating that in your thank-you email will let them know that *this* is the job that you want and that *this* is the station that you want to be a part of.

At the end of your interview, hopefully you asked when the employer was expecting to make a decision about who they were going to hire. If you haven't already heard from them within few days of that date, you should send another email or call, just to make sure they know as they make their final decision, that you are still interested.

One final thought: If you don't get the job that might not be the end of the story. First, it is very important to be gracious when you are given that information, even though it will be disappointing. Ask what qualities or skills the employer felt that you were lacking or needed to improve. And also, ask them to keep you in mind in case something else opens up at the station. You did a lot of work to get all the way to the interview process and that work just might pay off sometime down the line.

201

Becoming a Pro

You can also keep the lines of communication going very easily by dropping the person you interviewed a line when something happens in your career. Things like if you go back to school to work on your grad studies or you land your first job elsewhere. Drop them an email . . . or really surprise them and mail them a postcard or letter.

Sometimes letting an employer know that they let a good one get away can have some very welcome surprises.

Points to Remember

- Do your homework before your interview. Find out all you can about the station and about the person who will be interviewing you.

- Be prepared to demonstrate your skills again before or after your interview.

- Ask for the job! Let the person you are talking to know that you want to work at *that* station.

- Follow-up. Don't just wait for a call from the station. Be proactive and keep in touch with the person you interviewed with.

Exercises

1. Select a radio or television station in your area and research it as if you were preparing for an interview. Find out everything you can that might be useful if you were applying for a job there. Write a paper detailing your findings. Make sure to write it in conversational newswriting style.

2. Write a sample follow-up email that you could send to the station as a follow-up to your interview. Think about ways to keep yourself on top of their list of potential candidates and don't forget to let them know why you want the job.

> *Take great pride in what you do . . . your enthusiasm will show*
> *in your broadcasts . . . and people will take great interest.*
> —Mike Wagner – KFYR Bismarck, North Dakota

Making Your First Career Move

In this Chapter

- Research
- Geographical Considerations
- Unions, Agents and Managers

Once you land your first job, you can breathe a sigh of relief. You have started your career and are now a broadcasting professional. But don't get too comfortable. You are going to be starting over many, many times throughout your career.

It's easy getting very complacent and not wanting to go through the entire process and anxiety of interviewing for a new job at a different station and perhaps in an entirely different market. But that is how we advance our careers in this industry.

For most people, the time to make that first career move is six months to one year after they get their first job. Once you start working five days a week on your craft, your skills are going to improve very quickly. You are essentially going to 'outgrow' that job and in order to move up in the industry, you are going to have to start making an effort to get a job at a larger station that matches your new skill level.

Research

Just as you researched your first job, when the time is right, you will start researching your next job. It may be the station across town, but more likely it should be a station in a larger market than you are currently in.

Becoming a Pro

You'll want to look for a station that is not that dissimilar to your current station in terms of format or programming. This is the type of station where your skills are going to be the strongest and where you have already established yourself as a professional.

You have also already established a track record within that type of broadcasting, and if you are on-air talent, you should be able to show some ratings or records to bolster your self-promotion. Your station should have these and should be willing to make them available to you. Obviously you do not want to let the station know that you are looking to move on, but it's not that unusual for air talent to want to see their ratings. In fact, some managers consider that a part of the job. If you know where you stand in comparison with others in your position in the market, it will give you some guidelines into how you might be able to improve your performance.

Geographical Considerations

Not everyone wants to be in the top markets in the nation and that is ok. If you like the area or the lifestyle in a smaller market, then work to become tops in that market. Whatever works best for you is right. You don't have to pursue you career to anyone else's standards.

Moving from market to market is a double-edged sword in this industry. Some people look at it as a way to see cities and parts of the country that they wouldn't otherwise have a chance to see. Others look at it as a necessary evil in order to move up in the business and eventually make it to one of the major markets.

There are two ways to approach it but first let's make it clear that not everyone does move to a small town in order to start their careers. I started in Southern California right out of college and never left. My entire career has been and continues to be in the number two market in the country, the Los Angeles market. It is possible, it is just not probable. I consider myself extremely lucky. It is not something you should set your heart on doing because you are really limiting the number of stations that you can apply to and reducing the likelihood of being hired.

There are many job listing sites that you can check and find stations that are in the areas that you might be interested in. You can apply to any job that you feel suits your current skills. Or you can research stations

Making Your First Career Move

and apply directly to ones that you feel would simply be a good fit for you. Just because you do not see a job listing for that particular station does not mean they don't have any openings, you may simply not have found them. Give them a quick phone call and you might find that they are looking for someone exactly like you.

If this sounds like a lot of work, it is. But it is how you advance your career.

Unions, Agents and Managers

Let's start with a very important fact: You do not need to be in any of our unions or have an agent or manager to look for your first job. You may not need these things for quite some time.

There are plenty of people out there who will tell you differently and they usually want money up front to work with you. That should be a red flag that means *run*!

A legitimate agent or manager will not charge you for representation. They get paid when you work and will not take you on as a client unless you are ready to work.

You will be well along in your career before either of these people becomes an essential for you. Your early earnings will not be that great, so there is no need to give 15-percent to someone you really do not need and who cannot really do much for you either. The time to consider either of these professionals is when your career is well along, you are working in one of the larger markets and are making a significant amount of money.

Even if the first job you get is a union job, you do not have to already be in SAG-AFTRA when you apply or even if you get hired. You will have to join the union to work at the station, but most of the entertainment unions give you several weeks to join and will also work out a schedule of payments for your initiation fees and your dues.

You can always contact the local chapter of the union that would cover your area of work for advice. They will be genuine in their answer and will continue to be a good resource for you during your career. When you are ready for an agent, they will also be able to provide you with a list of what are called franchised agents who have agreed to a specific code of conduct with members of the union.

205

Points to Remember

- Your first job will not be your last job; you will likely change stations many times during your career.
- You should be ready to move on from your first job within six months to a year.
- You do not need to already be in SAG-AFTRA to apply at a union station.
- Any agent who asks you for money in order to represent you is unethical and you should not do business with them.

> *Get the information first but first get it right.*
> —John Brown – Retired Traffic Reporter/Meteorologist,
> Total Traffic and Weather Network

PART VIII

Conclusion

focal point/shutterstock.com

# Conclusion

In this Chapter

- Sense of Duty
- Pursuing Your Passion
- Rewards of Being a News Professional

You are about to enter one of the most exciting and rewarding parts of the broadcasting industry. It is also one that comes with a lot of responsibility.

Sense of Duty

The news you write or present on the air is going to be heard by hundreds, thousands or even millions of people. There is a level of credibility that people automatically assign to what and who they hear on the air. That is why you need to do everything possible to make sure that the stories you write are accurate and ethical.

Since the 2016 presidential election, much of the credibility of the news media has been seriously damaged. People have seen their careers damaged or even destroyed, some rightfully so. But the majority of the people in the news media are good, hardworking people who care a great deal about what they do. Unfortunately, the bad light that the current climate has put the news media in will take many years to correct and it has forever changed the industry.

All of this is compounded by the speed at which news and information is now generated and disseminated and the proliferation of information on

Conclusion

social media. The general public is not as savvy as it should be in validating information before passing it on, so it does not take much time for something that is erroneous to spread like wildfire.

Social media and the Internet have become sources, not just for the public but also for the news media. We need to be vigilant in our vetting of all information that we find online before using it in a story. We also need to provide attribution in our stories so that people can understand where the information we use comes from and hopefully feel assured that we are using credible sources.

Radio and television news will be the way that the majority of people get their information for a long time to come. We are the alternative to the faceless, voiceless, non-accountable Internet. We need to work to keep the public's confidence and understand that we have the honor of being the ones people know they can trust when they are trying to make sense of the world.

Pursuing Your Passion

Passion – it's defined as "a strong and barely controllable emotion". While that might be a bit dramatic, to be in this business, informing people needs to be your passion. You need to feel driven to let people know what is going on, to explain to them how the news affects them and at the same time, entertain them. You need to want to be the person that the audience turns to and believes in.

The confidence of your audience is a very valuable thing. If you can earn it and keep it, you will see the benefits in your ratings, your career progression and your life.

Rewards of Being a News Professional

Working in the media is a very rewarding career that makes all the work you are doing right now and the work that you will do in the future worth it. While working in this industry can mean long and crazy hours, low pay, relocating and often dealing with stressful situations and stories, you have the opportunity to improve and change people's lives . . . and maybe to even save a life.

Conclusion

You may get to meet people and go to places that most people only dream about. Once you are established and move to the larger markets, your pay may put you well above what the average person makes. And if fame is something that matters to you, that is something that also may come your way.

Over the years, I've often been asked what the most important story that I have ever done is. I have covered presidents, international leaders, earthquakes, riots and anchored during many national and world events and crises. But none of those are the stories that I cite when I am asked that question.

That story came during some incredible firestorms that we had in Southern California in the mid-1990s. Much of the beach community Malibu was on fire as the Santa Ana winds blew for several days. A similar fire was raging about 60 miles away through a beach colony in Orange County.

The radio station that I was on had been on wall-to-wall coverage for many hours. Everyone was doing everything; job designations didn't matter much at this point. I was in the newsroom and answered the phone. There was a man on the line who was simply yelling into the phone to the point that I could barely understand him. I had answered with my name so he knew who I was. But he didn't care. He wanted information. He had heard us give information out on the air several hours ago about a group that was helping to evacuate horses and he needed that information . . . now.

He said he could see the flames and they were coming straight toward his home and he vowed that if he could not evacuate his horses, he would not leave either. We scrambled and finally found the info he needed. I gave it to him and he hung up.

A week or so later, a call came into the newsroom for me. The man had called back. He told me that he had just been allowed back into his neighborhood and that his house was gone, burned to the ground. I started to tell him how sorry I was, but he interrupted me and said that he didn't care about his house. He and his horses were fine! The information I had given him that crazy day had allowed him to get the help he needed to get his horses and himself out in time. He said I had saved all their lives.

We were both crying by the time he said goodbye. I never got his name.

A small event in the bigger picture of the world. But to the man, his horses and me, the most important one of our lives.

Conclusion

Welcome to the news business. Remember how much influence you can have on people and how much good you can do. You're going to be great!

> There can be no greater credibility for you, than to be looking at what you are talking about. The next commandment is knowing your audience. Be it Radio, TV or Print/Social Media, you must know what your audience is doing or what they're about to do. In Los Angeles and most cities it's easy. If you're on the Radio, I'd guess 99% of the people listening to you are driving a car, truck or something with wheels. On TV, most are home and possibly about to leave home, at the office, school or wherever. As for Print/Social Media please, anything but NOT driving!! Once you've figured out the 'language' to use for your audience, after a while it will become natural to you. Just like talking on the phone with your friends telling them what you're going to do today. For instance . . . the early morning TV Traffic reporter that goes on air and says . . . "two lanes are blocked on the so and so Freeway and traffic is backed up for miles, use the so and so road instead", is no doubt giving out good information but means absolutely nothing to the single Mom, chasing young kids around the kitchen trying to get them ready for school and glancing at the morning News while doing so!! If perhaps you say to your TV single Mom . . . "If you are here and have to drive there!!! Don't take this freeway go this way." Now you're really helping someone!! On radio you can say things like . . . "this is happening, get off the freeway and do this" because chances are they just might be driving toward what you're talking about. When it comes to 'Breaking News', be you airborne, in studio, on TV or Radio, giving the exact information about the event is crucial but don't forget about the section of the audience that will soon be driving or already is driving to what you're reporting on. Imagine driving towards your home and hearing for the first time that a massive brush fire is blazing through your town. You'd want to know how to get there as fast as possible and

what to do once you got there. Always remember . . . "You"
is THE most important word in broadcasting!!! Talk to me!!
That's your job. Nothing like it!!! People will thank you!!
You'll sleep great at night!!!

—Jeff Baugh – Airborne Reporter, KFWB,
KNX, KFI, Los Angeles

About the Author

Tammy Trujillo is both an entertainer and an educator. She began in the entertainment field as a child and since graduating from Cal State Fullerton has continuously worked in the Los Angeles market as a News Anchor, Reporter, Sportscaster, Public Affairs Director and Commercial Voice Over Artist. Her list of credits includes some of the biggest stations in Southern California including KNX, KFWB, KFI, Power 106, KMPC and The Beat.

Combining her real-world experience with a hands-on approach to learning, Tammy has also taught broadcasting for the past 25 years at many of Southern California's most prestigious private schools and colleges. She is currently the lead Professor of Broadcasting at Mt. San Antonio College in Walnut, CA as well as Director of its two award-winning campus radio stations.

Throughout her career, she has received many honors for her work both on the air and behind the scenes, including numerous Golden Microphone Awards from the Radio Television News Association.

Tammy is a member of SAG-AFTRA, a former Board Member of the Associated Press Television and Radio Association, a Hall of Fame member at Long Beach City College and a member of Pacific Pioneer Broadcasters.

About the Author

Tammy Trujillo's first book, *Intern Insider – Getting the Most Out of Your Internship in the Entertainment Field*, is credited with helping many college students make that all important first step into the broadcasting industry.

Index

24/7 news cycle 49, 65, 71, 187–8

abbreviations 56–7
accountability 38–9
accuracy in news writing 32–3, 36–7, 75, 151, 155–6
acreage 58
acronyms 57–8: definition 53
actuality stories 78, 140–2, 144, 146–7: definition 76
addresses 58
advertising 161
agents 205–6
aggregators 153–4: definition 151
airlines 22, 52
airtime 28
Aldi, Roger 191
ambient sound 44, 93, 121, 125–6, 145: definition 138; use of 138, 144–5
analysis 94
anchor tag: definition 95, 138
animals 146–7: control of 96–100; large 133
answering the question 61–2
appearance 181–2; see also professionalism
area codes 131–2
A-Roll 143: definition 138
ascertained issues 108: definition 102; working with 102, 104
Associated Press (AP) 5, 13–14, 60, 67, 122–3, 139–40, 167–8: definition 9
astronomy 163
attitude and approach 173–8: changes during newscast 176–7; definition of 'attitude' 173; exercises 177–8;
industry vocabulary 173; points to remember 177
attribution 29–30, 32, 38, 93, 167, 210: definition 24
audience dynamics 50
audience needs 17–23: crisis and emergency 19–22; exercises 22–3; points to remember 22; relevance 90, 93; see also emergency situations
audio: cuts, definition of 121, 123; exercises 126–7; industry vocabulary 121–2; online 158, 159–60; points to remember 125–6; proper use of 121, 122; services 13–14; station-gathered 121, 124–5; types 121–7; wire-generated 121, 122–4
author biographies 153
avatars 66

background information 70
balanced: definition 34; see also fair and balanced reporting
banks 23
Baugh, Jeff 213
Beach Boys 33
Beard, John 147
Belzman, Gary 33
Bernsen, Rod 137
bias 16, 43, 94; see also unbiased reporting
blogs 25, 155–6, 166: definition 164
boringness 3, 6
branding 195–7
breaking news 188
B-Roll 121, 124–6, 143, 147: definition 121
Brooks, John 127

217

Index

Brown, John 206
brush fires 19–20, 45, 133, 212–13
bullet points: definition 128
Burli 14
business cards 196–7
business news 110, 114, 118

camera-ready 181: definition 179
Candy Lab 88
career moves 203–6: agents 205;
geographical considerations 204–5;
interview research 202; managers
205; points to remember 206;
research 203–4; unions 205
Cassidy, Jeff 142, 143
celebrity interviews 135
cellphones 18–20, 42, 164, 180, 193,
196–7
charities 105
children 39
citizen journalists 166: definition
164
citizenship rights 38
clarity 75; see also proof reading
climate change 52, 88
CNN 168
cold read: definition 173
collective nouns 64
command center: definition 128
commentary 94, 147
commercial endorsement 38
confidence 175, 210
content curation 152–3: definition
151
conversational: definition 53; style
156, 177, 202; word replacement
56, 63–4; writing 55–6
copy: definition 53, 65
copyright infringement 13–14, 122,
145, 168; see also fair use law
cover letters 192–4, 196–7
creating material 194
credibility 43, 156–7, 163, 165, 167,
174, 210, 212
crime stories 10–11, 91–2, 104, 109
critiquing 31
cut audio 140
cut from the bottom: definition 53, 54
cuts: finding the right 138, 139;
multiple 138, 144; writing in and
around for TV 138, 143–4; writing in
and out for radio 138, 140–3

Davis, Nichole 197
deadlines 44
death of prominent figures 177
death tolls 58, 86–7
deception 36
defamation 26–7, 32–3: definition 24
definitions of news 9–16
delivery 174–6
dementia 51
demo reel 194, 196, 200: creating and
marketing 192–7
demographics 50, 51, 93: definition 49
Deutsch, Linda 101
development of story 97
diets 163
digital editors 14
disasters see emergency situations
disclosure 37
discounts 38
distractions 69
domain names 153
'doom, gloom, death and destruction'
3, 4, 6, 10, 21, 86–7
Dow Jones: definition 110
dramatization 36
dress code 181–2
driving 52, 163, 212
drug use 104, 109
duty see sense of duty

earpieces 56
earthquakes 19, 22, 87, 211
Eastern Standard Time 114, 117
economic issues 104, 109
editorial: definition 34
editorializing 34, 43–5
editorials 40
editors 14
education 17, 19–21, 104, 109:
definition 17; educational purposes
31; educational stories 11
effective interviewing: industry
vocabulary 128–9; see also
interviews
EFX see sound effects
electronic media style 152
emails 4
emergency situations 19–22, 107–8,
169, 211
emotion 174, 177, 188–9, 210
employment 104, 109
endorsement 29, 38: definition 24

Index

ENPS 14
enterprising stories 90–4: definition 90; exercises 94; industry vocabulary 90–1; points to remember 93
entertainment stories 6, 17, 21: definition of 'entertainment' 17
enthusiasm 202
environmental issues 88, 104, 109
Equal Time rule 43
ESPN 168
ethical and moral newswriting 34–45, 134: ethical decision-making 44–5; ethical journalism 37, 39; exercises 44–5; industry vocabulary 34–5; points to remember 43
ethics: definition 34
evacuations 11, 19–20, 133, 211
expert interviews 98

Facebook 154, 163, 166, 195
fact reporting 94
fair and balanced reporting 34, 41
fair comment 27
fair use law 31–2, 145: fair use, definition of 24
fairness and balance 32, 33
fake news 34–5, 152: spotting sites 151, 153–4
false light 27–8: definition 24
family life 189–90
faxes 4
Federal Communications Commission (FCC) 28, 43, 106–8: requirements 102, 103
Federal Trade Commission (FTC) 29
feel-good stories 11
Final Cut Pro 196
finding ideas 90, 91–2
fire damage 72–3, 78–9
fire zone 133
firefighting 133, 141
firestorms 211
first responders 128, 135–7: definition 128
fleetingness 31
floods 19
follows: definition 76; see also to follows
follow-up interviews 201–2
follow-up questions 136: definition 128
food product recall 22

formatting stories 99
freebies 38
Fuller, Randy 89
fun stories 91

games 88; see also sport
Garcia, Sid 45
gas prices 51
general interest stories 10, 15
geographical considerations 204–5
gestures 175–6
gift-giving 38, 61
Gone With the Wind 145
Google 67, 154, 169
gossip 180
green light: definition 90
guests 102, 105

Hall, Jim 109
hand gestures 175–7
headlines 83–9: composition 85–6; definition 83; exercises 88–9; industry vocabulary 83–4; limitations 86–7; points to remember 87–8
headphones 56
health 104, 105, 109
hero stories 3
history 133
Hollywood 52
homelessness 104, 109
honesty 197
Hook, Marshall 82
housing 104, 109
human-interest stories 11, 21
humorous stories 11, 21
hyphenating 59

ideas see finding ideas
identification of minors 24, 30–1
identity protection 31
identity theft 45
'if it bleeds, it leads' 3
impartiality see unbiased reporting
incue: definition 138
independence: editorial 37–8
industry vocabulary: attitude and approach 173; audio and video 121–2; effective interviewing 128–9; enterprising stories 90–1; ethical and moral newswriting 34–5; headlines 83–4; interview clips 138–9;

219

Index

multi-media 158–9; multi-part stories 95; news judgment 49; newscasts 17–18; origins of news 9–10; professionalism 179–80; promos 83–4; public affairs 102–3; public service announcements 102–3; rewriting 65–6; rules and regulations 24–6; series creation 95; social media 164–6; teases 83–4; types of news 110–11; types of stories 76–7; writing for internet usage 151–2; writing the news 53–5; writing the news 53–5
information 17–18: definition 17
informative news 6, 11, 15
initials 57–8
Instagram 195
interactivity: definition 164
interesting news 6
international: definition 9
internet: outage 137; presence 195; service 19–20; usage, writing for 151–7
internships 180, 182–3, 192: definition 179
interview clips: exercises 146–7; industry vocabulary 138–9; points to remember 145; selecting and writing with 138–47
interviews 198–202: appropriate questions 42–3, 128, 132–4; asking hard questions 128, 134; being a successful interviewee 199–200; effective 128–37; exercises 135–7, 202; expert 98; follow-up communication 201–2; follow-up questions 136; getting information from 138, 144; getting too much information 128, 134–5; job research 202; making it interesting 128, 131–2; points to remember 135, 202; preparing for 102, 105–6, 128–30, 198–9; recordings 44
investigative reporting 94
iPhones 163
irrelevance 3, 5–6

jewellery 176
Jimenez, Bob 33
jobs see employment
Johnson, Bruce 143

Kamber, Dawn 75
Kelman, Lori 52
kicker stories 11, 15, 17, 21, 76, 80–1, 86: definition of 'kicker' 9, 76
KISS method 111

lead in 140, 144: definition 138
lead story 51, 85: definition 49
legal issues see rules and regulations
Leishser, John 45
length of stories 5
Leone, Gary 170
letters 4
libel 24–7: definition 25
life of news professionals 25–6, 187–90: exercises 190–1; points to remember 190
lifestyle 190
LinkedIn 195
links to other media 151, 154–5
Little, Chris 64
local: definition 9; news 5
lock-outs 142: definition 139
logos 196–7
Lyon, Mary 15

malice 27
man on the street (MOS) 76, 80–1: definition 76
managers 205
marketing 195–6
McKeown, Kevin 23
Means, Michael 147
medical breakthroughs 3, 11
Medicare 6, 50
Mendelson, Alan 183
meteorology 116; see also weather
microphones 161–2
minors see identification of minors
missing persons 45, 177
mistakes see proof reading
money 58
morality see ethical and moral newswriting
morals: definition 34
movies 52, 145
multi-media news 151: exercises 156–7, 162–3; industry vocabulary 158–9; packaging for 158–62; points to remember 156, 162; see also social media

220

Index

multi-part stories 95–101: industry vocabulary 95
multiple sides *see* writing multiple sides
multi-tasking 69
murder 30, 42
Murphy's Law 66: definition 65
music 31, 33, 74, 178

Nadel, Roger 23
names: correct usage of 111, 132, 180
NASA (National Aeronautics and Space Administration) 57, 64
NASDAQ (NAHZ-DAK) 114: definition 110
national: definition 9
natural disasters 12
natural sound *see* ambient sound
negativity 3–5, 86–7
new laws 10, 22, 52, 177
New York Stock Exchange (NYSE): definition 110
news cycle: definition 65
News Director 103, 142, 199
news judgment 49–52: definition 49; exercises 51–2; industry vocabulary 49; points to remember 51
news platforms 14
news tests 200–1; *see also* interviews
'News You Can Use' 6
NewsBoss 14
newscasts: industry vocabulary 17–18
non-profit groups 109
numbers 58

objectivity 33
Olsen, Ron 16
on-call 187–8
one-on-one delivery 174: definition 173
origins of news stories 5–6, 9–16: exercises 15–16; industry vocabulary 9–10; points to remember 14
outcue: definition 139
outlining the story 96–7

pace 176, 177
paraphrase 59–60, 64: definition 53
parental consent 31
parks 177
parody 31

passion 64, 94, 209–10
pension plans 52
personal choices 182; *see also* professionalism
personality traits 190–1
pharmaceutical drugs 52
phone numbers 58
phonetic representation 67
Photoshop 160
phrases 59
pictures 160, 162–3; *see also* stills
Piela, Alexander 118
piercings 182
plagiarism 168–70: definition 164
plugola 24–5, 28–9, 32, 61: definition 25
podcasts 159–63: definition 158
Pokémon Go 88
police officers 70–1
politics 10
positive news 3–4
post-show responsibilities 102, 106–7
power outage 137
presidential campaign (2016) 11–12, 35, 151–2, 209
press releases 14, 61, 105
Price, Rhett Samuel 157
privacy 39
privilege, legislative 27
professional courtesy 38
professional ethics 34–40
professionalism 17, 179–83: appearance 181–2; definition 179; exercises 182–3, 197; industry vocabulary 179–80; points to remember 182, 196; *see also* attitude and approach
profitability of news 11, 18–19, 50, 82
promos 83–9: composition 84; definition 83; exercises 88–9; industry vocabulary 83–4; limitations 86–7; points to remember 87–8
pronouncers 66–9, 74: definition 65
pronunciation 73, 75
proof reading 65, 69–71, 73
proper attribution 151, 154
property taxes 19, 22
props 174–6
ProTools 196
psychographics 51: definition 49
psychology of news 23, 165

221

Index

public affairs 102–9: exercises 109; industry vocabulary 102–3; points to remember 108–9
Public Affairs Programming: definition 102
Public File 102–4, 108: definition 103
Public Information Officer (PIO) 130, 135: definition 128
public service 45
Public Service Announcement (PSA) 102–9: definition 102; exercises 109; industry vocabulary 102–3; points to remember 108–9
Public Utilities Commission 131
punctuality 180

Quarterly Report 102–4, 108: definition 103
questions and answers (Q&As) 76, 80, 129: definition 77, 121, 123–4
quotes 30, 64, 136

radio stations 20–1
Radio Television Digital News Association (RTDNA) 34–6: Code of Ethics 36–40
raw sound: definition 121, 123
reactions to news 12–13
readers 76–7: definition 77
Reagan, Ronald 62
reax 76, 79: definition 77
recapping previous segments 99–100
Reed Walker, Ed 94
regions/regional: definition 9
relevancy 17–19: definition 17; relevance to the audience 90, 93
reliability 151, 155
relocating 189
reputation 155; *see also* slander
research 203–4
responsibility 151, 155
resumes 192–4, 196–7
Reuters 5, 13, 60, 167–8: definition 10
rewards of news writing 210–13
rewriting 65–75, 81–2: exercises 74–5; industry vocabulary 65–6; points to remember 73
right to a fair trial 39
road closures 19, 22
robbery 52, 58, 81–2, 177
Roberts, Brian 157
RSS feeds 162: definition 158

Rudman, Richard 137
rules and regulations 24–33: exercises 32–3; industry vocabulary 24–6; points to remember 32

safety tips 19
SAG-AFTRA 205–6
S-and-P-500 114: definition 110
Saturday Night Live 31
scener: definition 121, 123–4
school lunches 52
school shootings 45
scientific issues 88
seasonal change 163
sense of duty 209–10
September 11, 2001 (WTC attack) 18
series creation 95–101: exercises 101; industry vocabulary 95; points to remember 100–1
Shaw, Desmond 94
Shutterstock 162, 170
side: definition 65
sides 71–4
Sig Alert 114–15; definition 110
Six Degrees 165
slander 24–7: definition 25
slogans 197
smartphones 54, 160
social media 13, 18, 25, 35, 101, 105–7, 151–7, 159, 209–10: audio and video 122; career development 195–6, 199; definition 164; exercises 156–7, 169–70; explosion on 36; industry vocabulary 164–6; interviews 132; legal considerations 164, 168; as a news source 164–70; origins 165; points to remember 156, 169; promotion through 164, 168–9; role of 164, 166–7; validation and vetting of 164, 167–8
Social Media Anxiety Disorder 165
Social Media Syndrome 165
sound 93; *see also* ambient sound; raw sound
sound bite 76; *see also* actuality stories
sound effects (SFX) 139
'sound for the sake of sound' 122
sourcing the story 90, 92–3
spellings 75
sponsor-provided content 37, 103, 161
sport: news reports 66, 163, 110, 111–14, 117

Index

staging 36
statistical information 97
stills: definition 158; use of 158, 160
stock footage 27
Stock Market: definition 110
Stone, Samantha 163
storms 11
story board: definition 95; outlining the story 96–7; story development 97
story count: definition 95; purpose and benefits 95–6
story development 97
story formatting 99
story outline 96–7
story selection 49–50; *see also* news judgment
stress 188–9
style differences 151, 152
style points 56–60: definition 53; errors 64
subscribing stations 14
success stories 3
summary of the show 107
symbols 59

tablets 54
tattoos 182
taxation 28, 51, 146–7; *see also* property taxes
teases 83–9: composition 84; definition 83; exercises 88–9; industry vocabulary 83–4; limitations 86–7; points to remember 87–8
testimonial 29: definition 25
texting 4, 52, 163
'theater of the mind' 125
time 58; *see also* Eastern Standard Time; Equal Time rule; punctuality; Total Run Time (TRT)
titles 132
to follows 76, 78–9, 81, 96
topics 102, 105
Total Run Time (TRT) 142
traffic: reports 104–5, 109–10, 114–16, 118, 163, 212; violations 71
tragedy *see* victims
transparency 37–8
transportation 23
travel 189
trending 36

Trujillo, Tammy 142
Trump, Donald 62
trust 45
truth 36–7
TV series 163
Twitter 167, 195
types of news 10–12, 110–18: exercises 117–18; industry vocabulary 110–11; points to remember 117
types of stories 76–82: exercises 81–2; industry vocabulary 76–7; points to remember 81

unbiased: definition 34; reporting 34, 40
understanding the story 174
unions 205
user-generated content: definition 165

vacation 189
verbal storyboards 96, 101
vetting: content 152, 153, 155–6, 210; definition 165
victims 39, 43: of tragedy, treatment of 34, 41–3
video: exercises 126–7; online 158, 159–60; points to remember 125–6; proper use of 121, 122; services 13–14; station-gathered 121, 124–5; types 121–7; wire-generated 121, 122–4
viral news 36
voice cut stories: definition 77
voice over (VO) 143: definition 139
voicers: definition 122, 123–4
vowel sounds 68; *see also* pronouncers
vulnerable adults 39

Wagner, Mike 202
Water Cooler Story 21: definition 17
weather 12, 33, 110, 116–18, 133
web-based news 151–7
websites 25, 93, 101, 114–16, 152–6, 159, 194–5: career development 194–5; *see also* social media
weddings 52
Weinstein, Michael 178
Weird Al Yankovic 31
White House 12: Correspondent's Dinner 62

Index

'who cares' story 6
wild fires 11
Winslow, Steve 82
wire copy 60
wire services 13, 67, 116: definition 10
work-related information 180
World War II 18
wraps 76–8: definition 77, 122, 123–4
'Write Like You Talk' 55

writing: for internet usage 151–2; for time 76, 81; multiple sides 65, 71–3; style 5
writing the news 53–64: exercises 63–4; industry vocabulary 53–5; points to remember 63

years 58

zoos 52, 146–7, 177

Check out these other titles to help advance your career in broadcasting! Find these and more at Routledge.com.

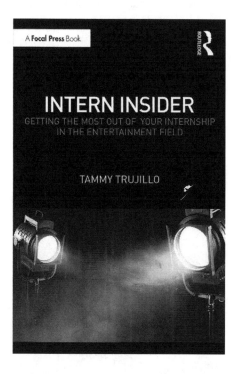

Intern Insider: Getting the Most Out of Your Internship in the Entertainment Field by Tammy Trujillo

Internships have all but became a requirement when starting out in the fields of entertainment and broadcasting. Students need these internships not only to get their foot in the door, but to gain valuable experience that gives them an advantage when going for that first job in the industry. *Intern Insider* helps students navigate the often daunting task of finding an internship, and equips readers to use the experience learned to begin a strong career in the entertainment world.

As both a professional broadcaster and college professor, author Tammy Trujillo approaches the topic of internships from both sides: what the student and intern site hope to gain. She provides various valuable perspectives throughout the book, including student assessments on their internship experiences, case studies of those who have turned their internships into careers, and interviews with internship site coordinators.

Her breadth of knowledge and experience make for a ground-level book both informative and useful.

In the competitive landscape of today's entertainment and broadcasting worlds, *Intern Insider* provides students with all the tools they need to make the most of their internships and jumpstart their careers.

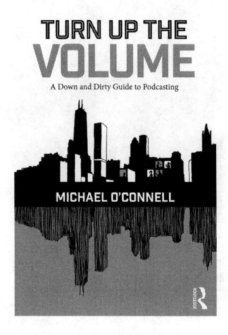

Turn Up the volume: A Down and Dirty Guide to Podcasting by Michael O'Connell

Turn Up the Volume equips journalism students, professionals, and others interested in producing audio content with the know-how necessary to launch a podcast for the first time. It addresses the unique challenges beginner podcasters face in producing professional level audio for online distribution. Beginners can learn how to handle the technical and conceptual challenges of launching, editing, and posting a podcast.

This book exposes readers to various techniques and formats available in podcasting. It includes the voices of industry experts as they recount their experiences producing their own podcasts and podcast content. It also examines how data analytics can help grow an audience and provide strategies for marketing and monetization. Written accessibly, *Turn Up the Volume* gives you a clear and detailed path to launching your first podcast.